KS2 SATs Practice Papers

8 English Grammar, Punctuation & Spelling Tests for Year 6

BUMPER COLLECTION
VOLUMES I & II

Ages 10-11

2020-2021 Edition

About this Book & How to Use It

Designed for Year 6 students, this book contains **8 complete, fully up-to-date** Grammar, Punctuation & Spelling Practice Tests, each of which is **closely modelled** on one of the **most recent** SATs Paper 1 exams — **including the 2019 exam**.

Like the actual exam, each Practice Test should be completed in **45 minutes** and consists of **46 to 50 questions** that assess the student's knowledge of English **grammar**, **punctuation** and **spelling**.

Also included for students are
◊ Practice **Cover Sheets**.
◊ Easy-to-understand **Instructions** providing information about the types of questions they will meet; the kinds of answers required; mark schemes; and time.

At the end of the book, parents and teachers will find
◊ The **complete Answers** for all four tests plus their **full Marking Guidelines**.

We recommend that
◊ Students attempt these tests in a **quiet environment**.
◊ Students work through these tests in order (as their **difficulty level increases**).
◊ These tests are used to **identify the areas** where students excel and those which they find challenging.
◊ The marks obtained by students in these tests are used as an **indication** of their progress.

Good luck!

Before you get started...

This book comes with FREE printable Self-Assessment Sheets and a List of Key SPaG Terms & Phrases for students.

To access them, simply visit our website @ https://bit.ly/2DVYoFk or use the QR code below:

Published by STP Books
An imprint of Swot Tots Publishing Ltd
Kemp House
152-160 City Road
London EC1V 2NX

www.swottotspublishing.com

Text, design, and layout © Swot Tots Publishing Ltd.

First published 2020.

Typeset, cover design, and inside concept design by Swot Tots Publishing Ltd.

British Library Cataloguing-in-Publication Data. A catalogue record for this book is available from the British Library.

ISBN 978-1-912956-28-9

CONTENTS

INSTRUCTIONS FOR STUDENTS

PLEASE READ THE FOLLOWING INSTRUCTIONS <u>CAREFULLY</u> BEFORE PROCEEDING WITH ANY OF THE PRACTICE TEST PAPERS IN THIS BOOK.

Questions & Answers

In each Practice Test Paper in this book, your grammar, punctuation and spelling are assessed. Each Paper contains different types of questions for you to answer in different ways.

Each question heading will make it clear to you what type of answer is needed, including the following:

- Multiple-Choice Answers
- Short Written Answers
- Ticking Boxes
- Circling or Underlining Words
- Connecting Boxes
- Filling in Boxes

Marks

Beside each question, on the right-hand side of the page, you will find a number followed by the words 'mark' or 'marks'. This tells you the maximum number of marks each answer is worth.

Time

You have 45 minutes to complete each Paper. Work through each Paper as quickly, but as carefully, as you can. If you finish before the 45 minutes are up, go back and check your work.

Good luck!

ENGLISH GRAMMAR, PUNCTUATION & SPELLING

PRACTICE TEST 1

FIRST NAME: _____

MIDDLE NAME: _____

LAST NAME: _____

DATE OF BIRTH: _____

SCHOOL NAME: _____

TOTAL SCORE: _____ / 50

1 Show which sentence must end with a **question mark**.

Tick one.

I asked how she had done that ☐

How did you do that ☐

Show me how to do that ☐

I want to know how you did that ☐

1 mark

2 Draw a line to connect each word to the correct **suffix**. You may use each suffix only once.

Word	Suffix
power	able
child	ment
comfort	less
amuse	hood

1 mark

3 Show whether each sentence is a **question** or a **command**. Tick one box in each row.

SENTENCE	Question	Command
Don't scare the birds		
Don't forget to feed the cat		
Don't you ever groom your pony		
Don't go near that dog		

1 mark

4 Insert one **comma** in the correct place in the following sentence.

Katy was late for school again so she began to run.

1 mark

5 Draw a line to connect each **prefix** to the correct word. You may use each prefix only once.

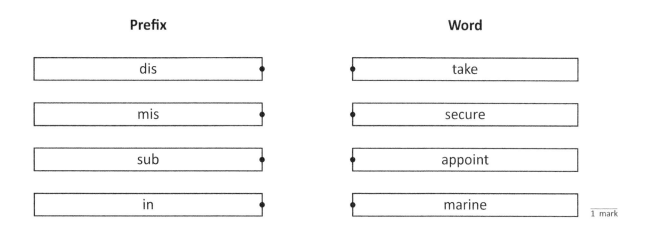

Prefix	Word
dis	take
mis	secure
sub	appoint
in	marine

1 mark

6 Show which sentence must **not** end with an **exclamation mark**.

Tick one.

What terrible weather we are having ☐

How cold it is today ☐

What an awful storm that was ☐

Make sure you take an umbrella ☐

1 mark

7 In each of the following, circle the word that completes the sentence so that it uses **Standard English**.

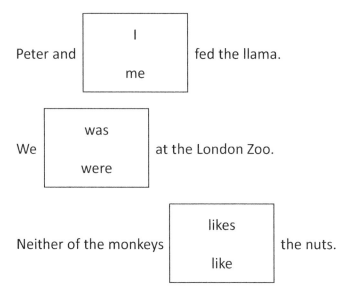

Peter and [I / me] fed the llama.

We [was / were] at the London Zoo.

Neither of the monkeys [likes / like] the nuts.

1 mark

8 Complete the following sentence by inserting a **relative pronoun**.

The film _____ I watched yesterday was exceedingly boring.

1 mark

9 Show which sentence uses the word <u>present</u> as a **verb**.

Tick one.

The mayor was <u>present</u> at the meeting today. ☐

The mayor is busy at <u>present</u>. ☐

The mayor gave his son a <u>present</u>. ☐

The mayor is going to <u>present</u> the prizes. ☐

1 mark

10 Insert a **semi-colon** in the correct place in the following sentence.

Jane wanted to play tennis her brother preferred to have a game of

squash.

1 mark

11 Insert a **pair of brackets** in the correct place in the following sentence.

The orang-utan one of the great apes is an endangered species.

1 mark

12 Show the meaning of the **prefix** <u>inter</u> in the words interfere, international and internet.

Tick one.

across ☐

between ☐

against ☐

distant ☐

1 mark

13 Show which sentence has been punctuated correctly.

Tick one.

Some tourists probably from Germany — asked me the way to the station. ☐

Some tourists — probably from Germany — asked me the way to the station. ☐

Some tourists — probably from Germany asked me — the way to the station. ☐

Some tourists probably — from Germany asked me the way to the station. ☐

1 mark

14 Identify the word that is a **synonym** of underlined deserted.

All the rats deserted the sinking ship.

Tick one.

boarded ☐

sailed ☐

abandoned ☐

crowded ☐

1 mark

15 Show which sentence is the most **formal**.

Tick one.

Would you care for another cup of tea? ☐

That was a lovely cup of tea, wasn't it? ☐

If I was you, I'd have a cup of tea. ☐

If you had asked, I would've made you a cuppa. ☐

1 mark

16 Show where a **hyphen** is needed in the following sentence. Tick one box.

Bernie had some carrot sticks, cherry tomatoes, a banana and a sugar free drink for lunch.

↑ ☐   ↑ ☐   ↑ ☐   ↑ ☐

1 mark

17 Identify the **word class** of <u>since</u> in the following sentence.

Martha has been absent from school <u>since</u> Wednesday.

Tick one.

a pronoun ☐

a conjunction ☐

a preposition ☐

an adjective ☐

1 mark

18 Circle the two words that are **synonyms** in the following passage.

There are many enthralling stories of the courageous deeds of King Arthur's knights. Perhaps the most valiant and chivalrous one of all was Sir Gawain.

1 mark

19 Name the kind of **clause** that is underlined in the following sentence.

As his sister was busy feeding the cat, <u>Suresh hid her phone under the sofa.</u>

_____

1 mark

20 Insert a **dash** in the correct place in the following sentence.

Nobody could find Jason he was hiding in the garden.

1 mark

21 Identify the **word class** of the underlined word.

Do you want pizza, <u>or</u> do your prefer lasagne?

Tick one.

a co-ordinating conjunction ☐

a subordinating conjunction ☐

a possessive pronoun ☐

a relative pronoun ☐

1 mark

22 Insert a **colon** in the correct place in the following sentence.

Aunt May refuses to go camping she is afraid of being bitten or stung by

insects or creepy crawlies.

1 mark

23 Insert three **commas** in the correct places in the following sentence.

Gerald enjoys swimming playing basketball rock climbing reading detective

novels and making models.

1 mark

24 Show which sentence uses **tense** correctly.

Tick one.

When Patrick says he has finished his homework, his mother looked surprised. ☐

When Patrick said he had finished his homework, his mother looks surprised. ☐

When Patrick had said he had finished his homework, his mother looks surprised. ☐

When Patrick said he had finished his homework, his mother looked surprised. ☐

1 mark

25 Draw a line under the sentence that is the most **formal** in the following passage.

Don't forget we're going on holiday next week! We're gonna have a whale of a time! Wish you could make it. I will call you on our return.

1 mark

26 Circle the word that shows that the following sentence is a **command**.

Please remain seated until the seatbelt sign is off.

1 mark

27 Use **(S) subject** or **(O) object** to label each box.

We haven't any cake left as Giles ate it all last night.

1 mark

28 Rewrite each of the underlined verbs in the **simple past**.

When Susie goes to the pool, she always swims ten lengths.

1 mark

29 Show which sentence is closest in meaning to the one below.

Danny can't go skiing because he has broken his leg.

Tick one.

Danny's leg is broken now. ☐

Danny broke his leg while skiing. ☐

Danny broke his leg last week. ☐

Danny is in hospital with a broken leg. ☐

1 mark

30 Circle the three **adjectives** in the following sentence.

Looking exhausted as he climbed the steep stairs, the lawyer seemed really unwell.

1 mark

31 Show which sentence is punctuated correctly.

Tick one.

Harry asked hopefully, "is there anything for supper?" ☐

Harry asked hopefully, "Is there anything for supper?" ☐

Harry asked hopefully, is there anything for supper." ☐

Harry asked hopefully "Is there anything for supper?" ☐

1 mark

32 Show which underlined word is an **adverb**.

Tick one.

The giant was huge and <u>ugly</u>. ☐

The monster glared with <u>hard</u>, angry eyes. ☐

The witch pretended to be <u>friendly</u>. ☐

The elves were <u>quite</u> peculiar. ☐

1 mark

33 Name the **word class** that the underlined words belong to.

We can go sledging <u>unless</u> it starts snowing again.

<u>If</u> it doesn't rain, we will go to the beach.

We can stay <u>until</u> the sun sets.

_____

1 mark

34 Explain how the position of the **comma** changes the meaning of the second sentence.

(i) Jan's aunt loves walking her dog and reading.

(ii) Jan's aunt loves walking, her dog and reading.

_____

_____

1 mark

35 In the following sentence, underline the **adverbial**.

The three friends agreed to meet outside the cinema.

1 mark

36 Complete the following sentence using a **relative clause**. Remember to punctuate your answer correctly.

The house, _____, was
extremely old.

1 mark

37 Explain how the **conjunction** changes the meaning of the second sentence.

(i) He began to complain after he drove home.

(ii) He began to complain as he drove home.

_____

_____

1 mark

38 In the following sentence, circle the **modal verb**.

Dad told Trish that she should share her toys with her brother.   1 mark

39 Rewrite the following sentence in the **passive**. Remember to punctuate your answer correctly.

The headmaster congratulated the winner of the competition.

_____   1 mark

40 Insert **two commas** and a **semi-colon** in the correct places in the following passage.

In the autumn the trees shed their leaves making a mess everywhere.

The gardeners have to work hard they go home exhausted every

evening.   1 mark

41 Circle the **three nouns** in the following sentence.

The   pianist   gave   a   brilliant   performance   last   night.

42 Show which sentence uses the **passive**.

Tick one.

The school team decided to enter the tournament. ☐

Every day, they practised hard. ☐

They were encouraged by their coach. ☐

Another team beat them in the final. ☐

1 mark

43 Write the **contracted form** of the underlined words in the following sentence in the box.

They <u>should have</u> tried harder!

↓

```
┌─────────────────────────┐
│                         │
│                         │
└─────────────────────────┘
```

1 mark

44 Complete the sentence below using a word formed from the root word <u>history</u> on each line.

In her work as a _____, Melinda has to read a great many

_____ documents.

1 mark

45 Write the grammatical term for the underlined words in the following sentence.

<u>The noisy magpies</u> have built a nest in the elm tree.

_____

46 Circle each word that should start with a **capital letter** in the following sentence.

in   december,   mr   mantovani   is   planning   to   go   to   manchester   to

do   his   christmas   shopping.

47 Circle the three **determiners** in the following sentence.

There   wasn't   much   fruit   left,   but   fortunately   I   found   two   pears

in   the   fruit   bowl.

48 Insert an **apostrophe** in the correct place in the following sentence.

The childrens books were on the shelves.

49 Circle the three **prepositions** in the following sentence.

The   library   is   at   the   end   of   the   corridor   opposite   the   stairs. $\overline{1\ \text{mark}}$

50 Circle the **co-ordinating conjunction** in the following sentence.

When   you   leave   your   office,   you   should   close   the   windows   and

turn   off   the   light. $\overline{1\ \text{mark}}$

END OF PRACTICE TEST PAPER 1

ENGLISH GRAMMAR, PUNCTUATION & SPELLING

PRACTICE TEST 2

FIRST NAME: _____

MIDDLE NAME: _____

LAST NAME: _____

DATE OF BIRTH: _____

SCHOOL NAME: _____

TOTAL SCORE: _____ / 50

1 Insert a **comma** in the correct place in the following sentence.

As Jeff was not answering his phone I decided not to buy him a ticket. ⎯1 mark⎯

2 Show which sentence must end with a **question mark**.

Tick one.

How this happens on a regular basis is a mystery ☐

I wish someone would tell me how regularly this happens ☐

How regularly does this happen ☐

There is no explanation as to why this happens regularly ☐ ⎯1 mark⎯

3 The prefix <u>mal-</u> can be used with the root word <u>function</u> to make the word **malfunction**. Tick the meaning of the word **malfunction**.

Tick one.

to fail to work ☐

to start to work ☐

to work quickly ☐

to work slowly ☐ ⎯1 mark⎯

4 Tick **one** box in each row to show whether the sentence is a **question**, a **statement** or a **command**.

SENTENCE	Question	Statement	Command
Iguanas are insectivorous lizards			
Do you know what 'insectivorous' means			
If you don't, look it up in a dictionary			
These lizards live in many tropical regions			

⎯1 mark⎯

5 Add two **commas** to the following sentence to make it clear Uncle Phillip loves four things.

Our Uncle Phillip loves rowing boats fishing and rivers.

1 mark

6 Tick the **adverb** in the following sentence.

Tick one.

Trish screamed loudly as the large, hairy, deadly spider crawled towards her.

□   □ □ □

1 mark

7 Insert a **pair of commas** in the correct place in the following sentence.

I've put the brown briefcase that smells a bit musty in the attic.

1 mark

8 Show which sentence is grammatically correct.

Tick one.

Last night, Iris gone to the theatre with her mother.   □

Three weeks ago, we had no idea this would happen.   □

In a couple of years' time, my brother will be go to university.   □

Next Monday, it had been a bank holiday.   □

1 mark

9 Show which word is a **synonym** of the verb <u>conflict</u>.

Tick one.

harm   □

ignore   □

shout   □

clash   □

1 mark

10 Identify the sentence that is a **command**.

You need to catch the 38 bus. ☐

Take the 38 bus to Olive Road. ☐

The 38 bus will take you to Dyne Road. ☐

I must catch the 38 bus in five minutes. ☐

1 mark

11 Draw a line to match each **prefix** to a word to make **four** different words. Use each prefix only once.

Prefix	Word
de	regard
em	port
dis	body
im	value

1 mark

12 Show which option completes the sentence in the **past perfect**.

They discovered their accountant _____ all their savings.

Tick one.

has stolen ☐

is stealing ☐

was stealing ☐

had stolen ☐

1 mark

13 Show which sentence is written in **Standard English**.

Tick one.

All the cold water in the fridge had been drunk. ☐

Kelly broughted her delicious tuna salad to the picnic. ☐

Yesterday, Thomas was been gone for hours. ☐

We was planning to visit Melissa last week. ☐

1 mark

14 Identify the sentence that uses a **dash** correctly.

Tick one.

Abi enjoys drawing — mandalas their intricate designs are very satisfying. ☐

Abi enjoys drawing mandalas — their intricate designs are very satisfying. ☐

Abi enjoys — drawing mandalas their intricate designs are very satisfying. ☐

Abi enjoys drawing mandalas their intricate designs are — very satisfying. ☐

1 mark

15 Identify the grammatical term for the underlined part of the sentence.

I bumped into Robert Mason <u>the other day</u>.

Tick one.

a main clause ☐

a subordinate clause ☐

a preposition phrase ☐

an adverbial ☐

1 mark

16 Show which sentence must **not** end with an **exclamation mark**.

Tick one.

How did you get here so quickly ☐

I can't believe how quickly you arrived ☐

How remarkably fast that was ☐

No-one has ever arrived so quickly ☐

1 mark

17 Insert a **colon** in the correct place in the following sentence.

The miser loved but two things his money and the vault that kept it safe. 1 mark

18 Show which sentence uses the underlined word as a **noun**.

Tick one.

Did Rachel <u>book</u> our tickets yesterday? ☐

The average number of hours an athlete <u>trains</u> will vary. ☐

I'm sorry I can't stop; I'm in a terrible <u>hurry</u>. ☐

I prefer <u>plain</u> bagels to those with raisins. ☐

1 mark

19 Show which sentence is punctuated correctly.

Tick one.

Suddenly, the temperature dropped rapidly and, our teeth began to chatter. ☐

Suddenly the temperature dropped, rapidly and our teeth began to chatter. ☐

Suddenly the temperature, dropped rapidly and, our teeth began, to chatter. ☐

Suddenly, the temperature dropped rapidly and our teeth began to chatter. ☐

1 mark

20 Explain how the use of the **modal verb** changes the meaning of the second sentence.

(a) Chris and Omar go scuba diving in Belize.

(b) Chris and Omar could go scuba diving in Belize.

_____

_____

_____ 1 mark

21 Identify the **word class** of the underlined word in the following sentence.

I haven't spoken to Jemma <u>since</u> her graduation ceremony last June.

Tick one.

adjective ☐

preposition ☐

conjunction ☐

adverb ☐ 1 mark

22 Insert a **subordinating conjunction** to show that they learnt about dolphins and were at the aquarium at the same time.

They learnt about dolphins _____ they were at the aquarium. 1 mark

23 Complete the following sentence with a **noun** formed from the verb <u>remove</u>.

The _____ of those recycling bins has been very unpopular. 1 mark

24 Replace the underlined words with the correct **pronoun**. Write one pronoun in each box.

Whenever I stay with my aunt, <u>my aunt</u> always makes delicious food. The last time I

[ ]

visited, however, I insisted that <u>my aunt and I</u> do something different. I took my aunt

[ ]

to a restaurant so that someone else could cook for <u>my aunt</u> for a change.

[ ]

1 mark

25 Show which sentence is the most **formal**.

Tick one.

Consulting the residents is probably a good move. ☐

We should consult the residents before we make our decision. ☐

The residents ought to be consulted before a decision is made. ☐

I think it would be a good idea to consult the residents first. ☐

1 mark

26 Barry wants to know where the meeting is being held. Write the **question** he could ask to find out. Remember to punctuate your sentence correctly.

_____

1 mark

27 Underline the **subject** of the following sentence.

Last Friday, a dangerous criminal escaped from a London prison.

1 mark

28 Write the name of the punctuation mark that could be used instead of commas in the following sentence.

Thankfully, within a few hours, the criminal was caught with the help of the public.

_____

29 Circle the most **formal** option in each of the following boxes to complete the advert.

Simon & Simon, your local travel agent, is

| proud |
| chuffed |
| well-pleased |

to unveil its most

| gobsmacking |
| amazing |
| mind-blowing |

holiday packages to date

for you and your

| mates |
| friends |
| besties |

this summer.

1 mark

30 Tick one box in each row to show whether the underlined noun is **singular** or **plural**.

SENTENCE	Singular	Plural
The firecrackers' explosions were ear-piercingly loud.		
That writer's horror stories are not as good as his detective novels.		
Mrs Lillian, our class's favourite teacher, is emigrating to Canada.		

1 mark

31 Write the **word class** of each underlined word in the spaces provided.

Rhonda always thinks <u>fast</u>. _____

Rhonda is a <u>fast</u> thinker. _____

1 mark

32 Show which sentence is the most **formal**.

Tick one.

If that sugar is left out, it will attract ants. ☐

Remember to buy a loaf of sourdough bread. ☐

He is training to become a heavyweight boxer. ☐

The manager insisted Tim be fired. ☐

1 mark

33 Circle the four **prepositions** in the following sentence.

In my opinion, it would be very silly indeed to go for a walk in this

torrential rain without an umbrella or a waterproof coat.

1 mark

34 Insert one **hyphen** and one **comma** in the correct places in the following sentence.

Helena's husband was an incredibly sociable good looking university lecturer.

1 mark

35 Explain how the position of the **apostrophe** changes the meaning of the second sentence.

(i) What are your student's most common mistakes?

(ii) What are your students' most common mistakes?

_____

_____

1 mark

36 Show which **two** sentences use punctuation to show **parenthesis**.

Tick two.

Despite the long queue, we waited to buy some delicious, Cornish pasties. ☐

Louis Pasteur, a French scientist, is regarded as one of the 3 founders of bacteriology. ☐

I find some fruit — particularly lychees, mangosteens and rambutans — rather odd. ☐

Unique to Mauritius, the dodo was a large, flightless bird — now long extinct. ☐

1 mark

37 Underline the **relative clause** in each of the following sentences.

The thieves needed a safe place where they could hide their loot.

A nonagon is a polygon which has nine sides.

Julia's pet hamster whose name is Squiggly always seems to be asleep.

1 mark

38 Rewrite the underlined verbs in the **simple past** tense.

Every summer holiday, the Thompson family go to the Lake District where they always

[ ]

have a wonderful time.

[ ]

1 mark

39 Name the grammatical term for the underlined words in the following sentence.

This is a treaty which will enable us to tackle global warming far more effectively.

_____

1 mark

40 Tick one box in each row to show whether the sentence is written in the **active** or the **passive**.

SENTENCE	Active	Passive
The results should be announced by 5 pm.		
Troops are being sent to the border.		
The temperature has dropped since yesterday.		

1 mark

41 Rewrite the sentence below as **direct speech**. Remember to punctuate your answer correctly.

They asked if they could have some more juice.

They asked, _____

1 mark

42 Circle the **possessive pronoun** in the following sentence.

Despite the three-day-delivery promise on your website, the cake tins that I

ordered from you two weeks ago still haven't arrived.

1 mark

43 Rewrite the two following sentences as one sentence using an appropriate **co-ordinating conjunction**. Remember to punctuate your answer correctly.

She was very late for her appointment. She was walking slowly.

_____

1 mark

44 Underline the **adverbial** in the following sentence.

We have been told the trial will start next Tuesday.

1 mark

45 Circle the **relative pronoun** in the following sentence.

Kyle who trains at our local gym every Thursday afternoon dislikes bananas. $\overline{\text{1 mark}}$

46 Add a **suffix** to the words in the boxes to complete the sentences below.

Please, be quiet: your whispering is unbelievably _____.

⬇

distract

This argument is too complex; you need to _____ it.

⬇

simple

$\overline{\text{1 mark}}$

47 Circle each word that should begin with a **capital letter** in the following sentence.

two of my favourite nursery rhyme characters used to be old king cole and

humpty dumpty. $\overline{\text{1 mark}}$

48 Circle the four **verbs** in the following passage.

There were several strange noises coming from the attic.

Bravely, Liam switched on his torch and headed towards the stairs. $\overline{\text{1 mark}}$

49 Rewrite the underlined verb in the following sentence so it is in the **present progressive**.

Unfortunately, we <u>experienced</u> difficulties with the website.

⬇

$\overline{\text{1 mark}}$

50 Underline the **subordinate clause** in the following sentence.

We were left speechless when we opened our front door: there was a

river of water streaming down our stairs.   1 mark

END OF PRACTICE TEST PAPER 2

ENGLISH GRAMMAR, PUNCTUATION & SPELLING

PRACTICE TEST 3

FIRST NAME: _____

MIDDLE NAME: _____

LAST NAME: _____

DATE OF BIRTH: _____

SCHOOL NAME: _____

TOTAL SCORE: _____ / 50

1 Draw a line to connect each word to the correct **suffix** so that it makes an **adjective**.

Word	Suffix
fiction	ive
expense	al
courage	ous

1 mark

2 Use the **conjunctions** from the box below to complete the following sentence. You may use each conjunction only **once**.

for	as	or

I could quite happily eat a whole pizza _____ a huge plate of pasta,

_____ I'm ravenous _____ I've not eaten since yesterday.

1 mark

3 Draw a circle around the **subject** in the following sentence.

Last week, poor Mrs Mitcham had a nasty accident in the street.

1 mark

4 Draw a line to connect each sentence to the correct **determiner**. You may use each determiner only **once**.

Sentence	Determiner
_____ cat killed the mouse.	an
Is there _____ explanation for this?	your
_____ guess is as good as mine.	neither

1 mark

5 Identify the option that must end with a **full stop**.

Tick one.

The train won't leave yet, will it ☐

When does this train normally leave ☐

Do you know if the train has left yet ☐

When the train will leave is not yet known ☐

1 mark

6 Show which sentence uses the **colon** correctly.

Tick one.

Helen has had several pets a cat: a gerbil a hedgehog a dog and a parrot. ☐

Helen has had several pets: a cat, a gerbil, a hedgehog, a dog and a parrot. ☐

Helen has had several pets a: cat, a gerbil, a hedgehog, a dog, and a parrot. ☐

Helen has had several: pets, a cat, a gerbil, a hedgehog, a dog and a parrot. ☐

1 mark

7 Use an appropriate **adverb** to complete the following sentence.

Rihanna is _____ late for meetings.

1 mark

8 Tick two boxes to identify where the missing **inverted commas** should go in the following sentence.

☐   ☐ ☐ ☐

Are you all going swimming? Molly asked.

1 mark

9 Put **one** comma in the correct place in the following sentence.

Quickly and quietly the thief moved around the empty house.

10 Tick one box in each row to show whether the sentence is in the **present perfect** or the **past perfect**.

SENTENCE	Present perfect	Past perfect
Anne has been our school librarian for a year now.		
She had worked at an investment company before that.		
She has seemed a lot happier since coming to the library.		

1 mark

11 Use the correct **pronouns** to replace the underlined words in the following sentences.

Last week, John decided to sell the old car that <u>John</u> had driven for twenty years.

Instead of replacing <u>the old car</u> with a newer one, John bought a bicycle.

1 mark

12 Show which sentence uses the **hyphen** correctly.

Tick one.

My seven-year-old brother is very naughty. ☐

My seven year-old-brother is very naughty. ☐

My seven year-old brother is very naughty. ☐

My seven-year old brother is very naughty. ☐

1 mark

13 Identify the sentence that shows it is **least likely** to snow tomorrow.

Tick one.

It shouldn't snow tomorrow. ☐

It mightn't snow tomorrow. ☐

It won't snow tomorrow. ☐

It mayn't snow tomorrow. ☐

1 mark

14 Draw a line to connect each sentence to its correct **function**. You may use each function only **once**.

Sentence   **Function**

| I want you to clean your grandfather's car this afternoon | command |

| Make sure that you remember to clean your grandfather's car today | exclamation |

| When are you going to clean your grandfather's car today | statement |

| How fantastically clean your grandfather's car looks now | question |

1 mark

15 Identify the sentence which is written in **Non-Standard** English.

Tick one.

The wizard had forgotten where he'd left his book of spells. ☐

I went to the mall at 4 o'clock and met my friends there. ☐

Sanjay and Anita didn't do their chores yesterday. ☐

They has bought her a wonderful birthday present. ☐

1 mark

16 (a) Identify the punctuation marks on either side of the words <u>quite remarkably</u> in the following sentence.

Despite the queue, we managed (quite remarkably) to buy some tickets.

_____

(b) Name a **different** punctuation mark which could be used correctly in the same places.

_____

17 Using the boxes given, write the **contracted forms** of the underlined words in each of the following sentences.

Their application <u>was not</u> accepted so <u>they are</u> going to reapply.

We <u>have</u> got loads of time before the flight — do not panic!

18 Your teacher is helping you to correct the punctuation of the sentence in the following box. Which **two** pieces of advice are you given?

"Where is the bus station" asked? the woman

Tick two.

There should be a question mark at the end of the sentence. ☐

There should be a full stop after the word 'station'. ☐

There should be a question mark after the word 'station', not 'asked'. ☐

There should be a comma before the word 'asked'. ☐

There should be a full stop at the end of the sentence. ☐

19 Show which sentence uses **capital letters** correctly.

Tick one.

Last September, a group of us went to the Greek island of Crete. ☐

Last September, a group of us went to the Greek Island of Crete. ☐

Last September, a group of us went to the greek island of Crete. ☐

Last September, a group of us went to the greek Island of Crete. ☐

1 mark

20 Insert a **semi-colon** in the correct place in the following sentence.

For years, the Browns never had much money that all changed when they

won the lottery.

1 mark

21 Show the meaning of the root <u>ject</u> in the word family below.

e**ject**ed   re**ject**ion   pro**ject**

Tick one.

refuse   ☐

area   ☐

stick   ☐

throw   ☐

1 mark

22 In the sentence below, circle the word that contains an **apostrophe** for **contraction**.

As they're all so muddy, Mary's boots, Jeremy's sneakers and Martin's shoes

must all be taken off before the children can come into Grandma's nice clean

house.

1 mark

23 Tick one box in each row to show if the **commas** have been used correctly in the sentence.

SENTENCE	Commas used correctly	Commas used incorrectly
For this recipe, you will need, sugar, flour, eggs, and maple syrup.		
A large number of animals, including lions, tigers, wolves and hyenas, are meat-eaters.		
Jonah has visited several places in Europe: Paris, Vienna, Madrid, Athens, and, Berlin.		
The laptop, which was very old, finally stopped working.		

1 mark

24 In the sentence below, circle all the **prepositions**.

Leaning   against   the   wall   stood   an   old,   wooden   ladder   under   which   was   a

rusty   bucket.

1 mark

25 Rearrange the words in the following statement to turn it into a question. Use the given words only. Make sure you punctuate your answer correctly.

Statement: The children have eaten their sandwiches.

Question: _____

1 mark

26 In the sentence below, circle the two words that show the **tense**.

Now,   we   have   a   house   in   Manchester,   but,   in   the   past,   we   lived   in   a   cottage

in   the   countryside.

1 mark

27 In each of the following sentences, underline the **main clause**.

Linda went for a walk in the park as it was warm and sunny.

If Gill doesn't arrive in the next five minutes, we're going home.

During the summer, while he was on holiday, Val broke his arm.

1 mark

28 Circle the **conjunction** in each of the following sentences.

Tom wanted to try bungee jumping although he knew it was dangerous.

Make sure you tidy up once you've finished in the art room.

1 mark

29 In each of the following, show whether the underlined clause is a **main clause** or a **subordinate clause** by ticking one box.

SENTENCE	Main clause	Subordinate clause
<u>The enemy spy waited patiently</u> until the sun had gone down.		
He walked in the shadows <u>as he did not want to be seen</u>.		
When he was sure the hangar was empty, <u>he crept inside</u>.		

1 mark

30 (a) Add a **comma** to the following sentence to make it clear that **only** Hal and Raj went to the shops.

Once they'd met Ed Hal and Raj went to the shops.

1 mark

(b) Add **commas** to the following sentence to make it clear that **all** three children went to the shops.

Once they'd met Ed Hal and Raj went to the shops.

1 mark

31 How do the different **prefixes** change the meanings of the two following sentences?

Kelly has <u>reread</u> the article.

This means that the article _____

_____

_____

Kelly has <u>misread</u> the article.

This means that the article _____

_____

_____

1 mark

32 Circle the two **prepositions** in the following sentence.

Boris, Brenda's cat, has broken the marble statuette which used to stand on

the small table outside her living room.

1 mark

33 Use the correct **possessive pronoun** to replace the underlined words in each of the following sentences.

These scissors belong to <u>my uncle</u>. They are _____.

These bicycles are owned by <u>my brother and sister</u>. They are _____.

Those shoes belong to <u>my mother</u>. They are _____.

1 mark

34 (a) Explain the meaning of the word **synonym**.

_____

_____

1 mark

(b) Write one word that is a **synonym** of the word <u>rational</u>.

_____

1 mark

35 Rewrite the verbs in the boxes below using the **present simple tense** to complete the following sentences.

This factory _____ very famous. It _____

| be |

| employ |

hundreds of workers and _____ Jaguars.

| manufacture |

1 mark

36 Using **adjectives** derived from the nouns in brackets, complete the following passage. One has been done for you.

Every year, the class choose Rosemary as their _____**favourite**_____ [favour] book monitor

because she is _____ [trust]. She is also extremely _____

[care] with everyone's books.

1 mark

37 Choose the option that completes the following sentence correctly.

That child _____ mother is a famous physicist has just won a science prize.

Tick one.

who's ☐

whose ☐

whom ☐

which ☐

1 mark

38 Use the word <u>break</u> as a **verb** in a sentence of your own. Do not change the word. Make sure you punctuate your sentence correctly.

_____

1 mark

Use the word <u>break</u> as a **noun** in a sentence of your own. Do not change the word. Make sure you punctuate your sentence correctly.

_____

1 mark

39 In the following sentence, underline the **relative clause**.

Catherine of Aragon who was born a Spanish princess was King Henry VIII's

first wife.

1 mark

40 Tick one box in each row to show if the sentence is written in the **active voice** or in the **passive voice**.

SENTENCE	Active voice	Passive voice
A gate was left open at the zoo.		
Some of the animals escaped.		
Luckily, they were all rounded up quickly.		

1 mark

41 Rewrite the following sentence so that it is written in the **passive voice**. Make sure you punctuate your sentence correctly.

A large, poisonous snake bit me.

_____

1 mark

42 Identify the two **adjectives** in the sentence below by drawing a circle around each one.

George rushed upstairs quickly to fetch his clean boots and a fresh T-shirt

from his bedroom.

1 mark

43 Select the option which shows how the underlined words in the following sentence are used.

<u>Fortunately for us</u>, in our village, there are several excellent restaurants.

	Tick one.
as a main clause	☐
as a preposition phrase	☐
as a noun phrase	☐
as a fronted adverbial	☐

1 mark

44 Select the verb that completes the sentence in the **subjunctive form**.

It was vital that the patient _____ treated at once.

	Tick one.
were	☐
be	☐
being	☐
was	☐

1 mark

45 Identify the function of the following sentence.

Come here at once and apologise

a command ☐

an exclamation ☐

a statement ☐

a question ☐

46 Show which sentence is written in the **past progressive form**.

Brushing your teeth last thing at night is a healthy habit. ☐

At the end of the holidays, we visited Jane in Dublin. ☐

The angry cyclist was shouting at the careless driver. ☐

I had to finish reading this book before the lesson. ☐

END OF PRACTICE TEST PAPER 3

ENGLISH GRAMMAR, PUNCTUATION & SPELLING

PRACTICE TEST 4

FIRST NAME: _____

MIDDLE NAME: _____

LAST NAME: _____

DATE OF BIRTH: _____

SCHOOL NAME: _____

TOTAL SCORE: _____ / 50

1 Identify the sentence that must end with a **question mark**.

Tick one.

When does the train depart ☐

He didn't know when the train left ☐

I asked Bruno when the train would leave ☐

Tell me when the train departs ☐

1 mark

2 Which **pair of verbs** completes the following sentence correctly?

One hundred years ago, computers _____ unheard of; now, however, they _____ an essential part of our everyday lives.

Tick one.

was   are   ☐

is   were   ☐

are   were   ☐

were   are   ☐

1 mark

3 Draw a line to match each **prefix** to the correct word so that it makes a new word.

Prefix	Word
ir	accurate
il	national
sub	legal
inter	responsible
in	marine

1 mark

4 Which sentence is punctuated correctly?

Tick one.

All around, her she could see a glistening blanket of snow. ☐

All around her she could see, a glistening blanket of snow. ☐

All around her, she could see a glistening blanket of snow. ☐

All around her she could, see a glistening blanket of snow. ☐

1 mark

5 Which of the following sentences is written in the **past tense**?

Tick one.

That beautiful painting is a self-portrait. ☐

It was completed in the nineteenth century. ☐

It is believed to be very valuable. ☐

It portrays its artist: a Frenchman. ☐

1 mark

6 Circle one word in each underlined pair to complete the sentences below using **Standard English**.

They **was / were** waiting for the bus for ages.

It **was / were** half an hour late.

1 mark

7 In the box, write the **contracted form** of the underlined words.

Ed <u>should have</u> arrived by now.

⬇

☐

1 mark

8 Identify the sentence that must end with an **exclamation mark**.

Tick one.

The team were badly beaten, weren't they ☐

I'll tell you why they lost ☐

Ask the manager why they didn't win ☐

What a terrible defeat for the team ☐

1 mark

9 Which sentence below uses an **apostrophe** correctly?

Tick one.

Owing to the storm, people's houses were damaged. ☐

Owing to the storm, peoples house's were damaged. ☐

Owing to the storm, peoples' houses were damaged. ☐

Owing to the storm, peoples houses' were damaged. ☐

1 mark

10 What does the word <u>few</u> refer to in the following passage?

The majority of birds in the British Isles are active during the day. However, a <u>few</u>, such as owls and nightjars, are nocturnal.

Tick one.

owls ☐

birds ☐

nightjars ☐

Isles ☐

1 mark

11 Circle **all** the **pronouns** in the following sentence.

Last week, Danny borrowed my calculator for his maths exam; irritatingly, he

broke it.

1 mark

12 Complete the following sentence with an **adverb** formed from the noun <u>conscience</u>.

Bob is a reliable worker and can be trusted to carry out his work

_____.

1 mark

13 Tick one box to show which part of the sentence is a **relative clause**.

The talented mechanic who repaired my car used to work in Germany.

☐   ☐   ☐   ☐

1 mark

14 Select the option that shows **how** the underlined words are used in the sentence.

After looking for two hours, Adam found <u>his missing textbook</u> under his bed.

Tick one.

as a main clause ☐

as a noun phrase ☐

as a relative clause ☐

as a preposition phrase ☐

1 mark

15 Tick one box in each row to show how **the modal verb** affects the **meaning** of each sentence.

SENTENCE	Modal verb indicates **certainty**	Modal verb indicates **possibility**
Maurice, my cousin, can speak French and Spanish.		
As odd as I know it sounds, that story could be true.		
Jim might be asleep now as he woke up at 6 am.		
I will apologise to Iris for shouting at her yesterday.		

1 mark

16 Name the **punctuation mark** used between the two main clauses.

Unfortunately, as she is not in school today, the headmistress, Mrs Priya Singh, cannot see you: she is attending a conference in Bristol for head teachers.

_____

1 mark

17 Tick one box in each row to show whether the underlined clause is a **main clause** OR a **subordinate clause**.

SENTENCE	Main clause	Subordinate clause
<u>Even though Jennie was good at rounders</u>, she preferred tennis.		
She played at the weekends <u>whenever it was possible</u>.		
Her father, <u>who coached her</u>, had been a professional player.		

1 mark

18 Circle **all** the **conjunctions** in the following sentences.

As I had to travel to Edinburgh for work, I decided to take the overnight train on Sunday evening.

When I checked the website, I discovered many of the trains to Scotland had been cancelled.

This made me delay my journey until the trains began running normally again on Monday.

1 mark

19 Circle the two words in the following sentence that are **synonyms** of each other.

Sir Gavin was rewarded with great riches for his bravery, for, as the king told him, he admired the courage that Sir Gavin had displayed in protecting the young prince from the giant.

1 mark

20 Tick **all** the sentences that contain **a preposition**.

The soldiers fought hard, but lost the battle. ☐

We've been waiting since six o'clock. ☐

As they watched the match, it began snowing. ☐

Pip became upset after he arrived. ☐

1 mark

21 Write a sentence that uses the word <u>promise</u> as a **noun**. Remember to punctuate your sentence correctly.

_____

Write a sentence that uses the word <u>promise</u> as a **verb**. Remember to punctuate your sentence correctly.

_____

2 marks

22 In the word family below, what does the root <u>spect</u> mean?

inspection   spectator   spectacles

Tick one.

look   ☐

test   ☐

correct   ☐

show   ☐

1 mark

23 Draw a line to match each word to its correct **antonym**.

Word   **Antonym**

| liberate | | genuine |

| responsible | | undependable |

| insincere | | hinder |

| assist | | confine |

1 mark

24 Rewrite the following sentence, adding a **subordinate clause**. Remember to punctuate your sentence correctly.

Louise and Jo swam in the sea.

_____

1 mark

25 Label the boxes below with **V (verb)**, **S (subject)** and **O (object)** to show the parts of the sentence.

<u>Sandra</u> baked a cake and <u>gave</u> <u>it</u> to her grandmother.

☐   ☐ ☐

1 mark

26 Circle all the words in the following sentences that should start with a **capital letter**.

marie is french, but she also speaks german. she has lived in berlin since

april, 2012.

1 mark

27 Which sentence below is written in the **active voice**?

Tick one.

The customer has been given a free meal.   ☐

The slippery road caused an accident.   ☐

All the work was done by robots.   ☐

Our luggage was sent to India by mistake.   ☐

1 mark

28 Which sentence below is punctuated correctly?

Tick one.

The play was very good brilliant, in fact, so it was no surprise that the audience applauded loudly. ☐

The play was very good — brilliant, in fact, so it was no surprise that the audience applauded loudly. ☐

The play was very good — brilliant, in fact — so it was no surprise that the audience applauded loudly. ☐

The play was very good — brilliant, in fact, — so it was no surprise that the audience applauded loudly. ☐ 1 mark

29 Tick one box to show where **a dash** should go in the following sentence.

The team knew exactly what would happen their striker would be sent off.

↑ ↑ ↑ ↑
☐ ☐ ☐ ☐

1 mark

30 Tick one box to show which sentence below uses the **present perfect**.

Tick one.

Claire has visited Greece several times. ☐

The tourists all went diving in the Aegean. ☐

After he had arrived in Athens, Sanjeev visited the Acropolis. ☐

Declan had been studying the ancient Greeks for years. ☐ 1 mark

31 Which of the following sentences is a **command**?

Tick one.

We could go and have a coffee and a muffin. ☐

They had better take the rubbish out. ☐

There's a new novel you really should read. ☐

When you see Jake, tell him about the party. ☐ 1 mark

32 Rewrite the following sentence as **direct speech**. Remember to punctuate your answer correctly.

Mike informed Janet that he knew where her book had been left.

Mike informed Janet, _____

_____

1 mark

33 Insert a pair of **commas** in the correct place in the following sentence.

One of the five retired racehorses which were being auctioned last weekend

won the Grand National ten years ago.

1 mark

34 Tick one box in each row to show whether the underlined word is **an adjective** OR **an adverb**.

SENTENCE	Adjective	Adverb
I will see you <u>later</u>.		
I'm wearing my <u>best</u> jacket.		
The bird sang <u>sweetly</u>.		
The girl was <u>lonely</u>.		

1 mark

35 Explain how the use of the **commas** changes the meaning in these two sentences.

The children, who were in Year 6, received prizes.

The children who were in Year 6 received prizes.

_____

_____

_____

1 mark

36 Which sentence below uses the **hyphen** correctly?

Tick one.

I have an up to-date version of that software. ☐

I have an up-to-date-version of that software. ☐

I have an up-to-date version of that software. ☐

I have an up-to date version of that software. ☐

1 mark

37 Rewrite the following sentence so that it is written in the **passive voice**. Remember to punctuate your answer correctly.

The angry bull chased them across the field.

_____

1 mark

38 Tick one box in each row to show if the word **until** is **a preposition** or **a subordinating conjunction**.

SENTENCE	**until** used as a preposition	**until** used as a subordinating conjunction
She can't go to school <u>until</u> she has completely recovered.		
You must wait here <u>until</u> the doctor can see you.		
He is going to be busy <u>until</u> the end of the month.		

1 mark

39 Complete the following table by adding a **suffix** to each noun to make an **adjective**.

Noun	Adjective
truth	
coward	
debate	
feather	
man	

1 mark

40 Tick one box in each row to show whether the underlined conjunction is a **subordinating conjunction** or a **co-ordinating conjunction**.

SENTENCE	Subordinating conjunction	Co-ordinating conjunction
Polly remained calm <u>although</u> I let out a blood-curdling scream.		
<u>When</u> I was finally able to speak, Polly asked me what was wrong.		
When I looked at her, I saw that she was smiling, <u>so</u> I stopped feeling guilty.		

1 mark

41 Complete the following sentence so that it uses the **subjunctive form**.

Is it necessary that she _____ there?

1 mark

42 Circle **all** the **determiners** in the following sentence.

Ten soldiers marched back to their camp early this morning.

1 mark

43 Underline the longest possible **noun phrase** in the following sentence.

The cunning thief denied that he had stolen all of Lady Herbert's valuable

paintings and jewels.

1 mark

44 Underline the **verb form** that is in the **present perfect** in the following passage.

Pompeii, in Southern Italy, was buried in ash when Mount Vesuvius erupted

in A.D. 79. Today, it has become an important tourist attraction that is visited

by thousands of people who want to see how the ancient Romans lived.

1 mark

45 Write a sentence that lists all the information given in the following box. Remember to punctuate your answer correctly.

To make a kite
a heavy-duty plastic bag
electrical tape
a line
a plastic winder
2 rods

_____

_____

_____

_____

_____

_____

1 mark

46 Complete the following sentence with a **possessive pronoun**.

Sally is a friend of _____.

1 mark

47 Circle the **adverb** in the following sentence.

Delia often meets her friends at the local sports centre after school.

1 mark

48 Insert a **colon** in the correct place in the following sentence.

That author's books are always exciting each one she has written is full of

thrilling adventures.

1 mark

49 Which **punctuation mark** should be used in the place indicated by the arrow?

When we decided to have a barbecue, we invited Mr Brown and his son, John Paul was
asked to come as well.   ↑

Tick one.

question mark   ☐

ellipsis   ☐

comma   ☐

full stop   ☐

1 mark

END OF PRACTICE TEST PAPER 4

ENGLISH GRAMMAR, PUNCTUATION & SPELLING

PRACTICE TEST 5

First name: _____

Middle name: _____

Last name: _____

Date of birth: _____

School name: _____

Total score: _____ / 50

1 Identify the sentence that must end with a **question mark**.

Tick one.

She didn't know where to go last night ☐

Where did she go Tuesday before last ☐

Ask Sally where she went on Monday ☐

Where she went last week isn't important ☐

1 mark

2 Insert a **semi-colon** in the correct place in the following sentence.

I must admit that I find geography rather boring history is far more interesting.

1 mark

3 Identify the sentence that uses **capital letters** correctly.

Tick one.

when Ali came to London, he visited Hampton Court. ☐

When ali came to London, he visited Hampton Court. ☐

When Ali came to London, he visited Hampton court. ☐

When Ali came to London, he visited Hampton Court. ☐

1 mark

4 The **prefix** co- can be used with the word operate to make the word co-operate. What does the word **co-operate** mean?

Tick one.

to work slowly ☐

to work separately ☐

to work together ☐

to work hard ☐

1 mark

5 Identify the **verb form** that completes the sentence correctly.

When Patrick _____ cooking, he always takes the rubbish out to the bins.

Tick one.

is finishing ☐

was finishing ☐

has finished ☐

has been finishing ☐

1 mark

6 Complete the following sentences by circling the correct **verb form** in each underlined pair.

At the end of next term, we **is / are** putting on a play at school.

I **is / am** playing the part of a soldier.

Ivy and Nesrine, my best friend, **is / are** in charge of the costumes.

1 mark

7 Select the option that completes the following sentence correctly.

_____ studied extremely hard for our exams.

Tick one.

Last year, all of my classmates and I ☐

Last year all of my classmates, and I ☐

Last year, all of my classmates, and I ☐

Last year, all of my classmates and I, ☐

1 mark

8 Identify the sentence that is correctly punctuated.

Tick one.

The rise of the robots a dire consequence — foreseen by the Professor — happened more swiftly than anticipated. ☐

The rise of the robots — a dire consequence foreseen by the Professor — happened more swiftly than anticipated. ☐

The rise of the robots, a dire consequence foreseen by the Professor — happened more swiftly than anticipated. ☐

The rise of the robots a dire consequence — foreseen by the Professor happened — more swiftly than anticipated. ☐
1 mark

9 Identify the **word class** of the underlined word in the following sentence.

"I can't answer <u>any</u> questions in this quiz," wailed Samantha.

Tick one.

subordinating conjunction ☐

preposition ☐

co-ordinating conjunction ☐

determiner ☐
1 mark

10 Tick one box to identify the correct place for a **dash** in the following sentence.

We finally learned the secret that the old beggar had kept hidden ↑☐ ... ↑☐

so well he was a very rich man.
↑☐ ↑☐

1 mark

11 Identify the **word class** of the underlined words in the following sentence.

Dom is <u>odd</u>: he speaks in a <u>soft</u> voice, but he has a <u>loud</u> laugh.

Tick one.

nouns ☐

adverbs ☐

determiners ☐

adjectives ☐

1 mark

12 Identify the sentence that is correctly punctuated.

Tick one.

Polly sneezed as she pulled down the box it was covered with dust: and cobwebs. ☐

Polly sneezed: as she pulled down the box it was covered with dust and cobwebs. ☐

Polly sneezed as she pulled down the box it was covered: with dust and cobwebs. ☐

Polly sneezed as she pulled down the box: it was covered with dust and cobwebs. ☐

1 mark

13 Identify the sentence that uses the word <u>fast</u> as an **adjective**.

Tick one.

I can't walk very <u>fast</u>; I've hurt my knee. ☐

That is a particularly <u>fast</u> sports car. ☐

The holy man decided to <u>fast</u> for two weeks. ☐

This is useless; we're getting nowhere <u>fast</u>. ☐

1 mark

14 Identify the sentence that is correctly punctuated.

The nearest city San Paolo is (two hours) away. ☐

The nearest (city) San Paolo is two hours away. ☐

The nearest city (San Paolo) is two hours away. ☐

The (nearest city) San Paolo is two hours away. ☐

1 mark

15 Identify the sentence that uses **capital letters** correctly.

Tick one.

Helen's great-grandfather fought in World War II. ☐

The local Museum is holding an interesting exhibition. ☐

My cousin works for a famous Computer Company. ☐

Many Gods were worshipped in ancient Rome. ☐

1 mark

16 Use an appropriate **subordinating conjunction** to complete the sentence below.

I never go swimming _____ I've had a heavy meal.

1 mark

17 Identify the sentence that is an **exclamation**.

Tick one.

The idea was utterly ridiculous ☐

She often has ridiculous ideas ☐

What ridiculous idea did he have ☐

What a ridiculous idea to have ☐

1 mark

18 Show which sentence uses the word <u>right</u> as a **noun**.

A <u>right</u> angle is always ninety degrees. ☐

"You have no <u>right</u> to say that!" exclaimed Cyril. ☐

Turn <u>right</u> at the next corner and follow the road to the end. ☐

"Your room is a <u>right</u> mess," complained Lily's mother. ☐

1 mark

19 Insert a **pair of brackets** in the correct place in the following sentence.

Selma whose two brothers joined our school has just started training

to become a dental surgeon.

1 mark

20 Use the correct **pronouns** to replace the underlined words in the following passage.

Last week, Bill and Ben lost their pet turtle, Ralph. <u>Bill and Ben</u> had to search for over

five hours to find <u>Ralph</u>.

1 mark

21 Identify the sentence that is correctly punctuated.

Tick one.

Sheila asked Hassan "Do you like that Renaissance painting?" ☐

Sheila asked Hassan: "Do you like that Renaissance painting"? ☐

Sheila asked Hassan, "Do you like that Renaissance painting?" ☐

Sheila asked Hassan, "do you like that Renaissance painting?" ☐

1 mark

22 Identify the most **formal** sentence below.

Tick one.

If only Juan were here, he would know what to do. ☐

D'you think Juan would know what to do? ☐

Juan would definitely know what to do — he's brilliant! ☐

Juan's always got a great solution up his sleeve. ☐

1 mark

23 Show which underlined group of words forms a **relative clause**.

Tick one.

"Who was at the door?" inquired Mrs Jenkins. ☐

If you know who stole the car, you should tell the police. ☐

I can't start cooking until I know who is coming to dinner. ☐

Phoebe who sings in the choir lives on my road. ☐

1 mark

24 In the sentence below, circle the two words that are **synonyms**.

The heat made them feel so lazy that they decided to have an idle

afternoon on the beach and do nothing other than relax and sunbathe. 1 mark

25 Tick one box in each row to show whether the apostrophe is used for **possession** or for a **contracted form**.

SENTENCE	Apostrophe used for possession	Apostrophe used for a contracted form
It's really cold today!		
Do not draw on the book's cover.		
Have you seen Noel's bag?		
I think that's the correct answer.		

1 mark

26 Show which sentence contains a **subordinate clause**.

Tick one.

Before dark, all the villagers had locked their doors. ☐

The dragon (the last of his kind) lived in the Misty Mountains. ☐

You're not leaving the table until you've finished your food! ☐

Rhoda's friends asked her for her sensible advice. ☐

1 mark

27 Show which sentence below is a **command**.

Tick one.

You haven't read that book, have you ☐

I wanted to know which book you liked ☐

She asked him where he bought his book ☐

Read all of this book by the beginning of next term ☐

1 mark

28 Insert **capital letters** and **full stops** in the following passage so that it is correctly punctuated.

Dervla murphy is an irish travel writer who has always been fascinated

by distant lands she cycled around the irish countryside when she

was young she has now visited places much farther away, including

ethiopia and peru

1 mark

29 Insert a **pair of commas** in the correct place in the following sentence.

Firemen who rescue people trapped in buildings are extremely brave

and deserve all our gratitude.

1 mark

30 Rewrite the verbs in the boxes below using the correct **tense** to complete the sentences.

My mother is the one who usually _____ what's for dinner.

| to decide |

Last year, the mayor officially _____ the new leisure centre.

| to open |

1 mark

31 Write a **command** which could be the first step in the instructions for cooking spaghetti. Make sure you punctuate your answer correctly.

_____

1 mark

32 In the following sentence, identify each of the clauses as either **main (M)** or **subordinate (S)**.

After they came top of their year, Layla started studying at university and

Paulina got a job working for a famous tech company.

1 mark

33 In each of the following sentences, circle the **conjunction**.

Arvind does not ride horses or play netball.

Although he enjoys rugby, Arvind does not like football.

If he tried tennis, I'm sure he would enjoy it.

1 mark

34 Show which two sentences contain a **preposition.**

Tick two.

Kenneth raced down the stairs. ☐

Yesterday, we went to our favourite cinema. ☐

Make sure you buy some butter tomorrow. ☐

Before he left, he thanked us. ☐

35 Identify the **object** of the following sentence.

On Sunday afternoon, Hans fed the ducks in the park.

Tick one.

Hans ☐

park ☐

ducks ☐

Sunday ☐

36 Insert a **comma** and a **dash** in the correct places in the following sentence.

Two Saturdays ago we watched an extremely exciting match between

Everton and Liverpool the last of the season.

37 Circle the **relative pronoun** in the following sentence.

The old man, who lived in a tiny cottage at the edge of the

forest, watched his dog as it played with its ball in the sunshine.

38 Rewrite the verbs in the boxes below using the **present simple tense** to complete the following sentence.

The young boy _____ very obedient and always

| to be |

_____ what his parents and teachers _____ him.

| to do | | to tell |

39 Insert a **pair of dashes** in the correct place in the following sentence.

Most   of   the   books   on   this   bookshelf   all   the   ones   about   ancient

Greece   belong   to   my   sister   Celia.

40 Identify the one **prefix** which can be added to all three of the following words to make their antonyms. Write your answer in the box.

honest
pleased
enchanted

41 Circle the two words that are **antonyms** in the following passage.

Tomas   was   more   than   willing   to   confess   that   he'd   eaten   all   the

biscuits.   However,   when   asked   about   the   cake,   he   was   reluctant   to

admit   to   having   consumed   that   as   well.

42 Circle the **possessive pronoun** in the following passage.

Rita showed me the new winter coat that she bought last week

in the sale. However, while it is nice, I don't think it's as nice

as mine.

1 mark

43 Identify which **punctuation mark** should be used in the place indicated by the arrow.

"Where have you been?" she asked Robin was not expecting to be questioned.

↑

Tick one.

comma ☐

exclamation mark ☐

question mark ☐

full stop ☐

1 mark

44 Use a word formed from the root word <u>friend</u> to complete each of the following sentences.

The large _____ dog wagged its tail when it saw me.

The fairy was delighted by her new _____ with the elf.

1 mark

45 Use a **verb** formed from the noun <u>exaggeration</u> to complete the following sentence.

I don't believe Sonia's story as she tends to _____ everything.

1 mark

46 Insert **two hyphens** in the correct places in the following sentence.

The brilliant concert pianist Anita Jacobs who is famous all over the

world also happens to be my aunt's sister in law.   1 mark

47 Rewrite the following sentence in the **passive voice**. Make sure you punctuate your answer correctly.

The gardener was watering the exotic flowers.

_____
                                                                    1 mark

48 Rewrite the verbs that are underlined in the following sentences so that they are in the **present perfect simple** form.

The fans <u>had enjoyed</u> the match immensely. It <u>had been</u> very exciting.

                                                                    1 mark

49 Complete the following sentence using a **noun phrase** containing at least three words. Make sure you punctuate your answer correctly.

_____ cheered wildly

when they saw the famous film star.   1 mark

50 Circle the **adverb** in the following sentence.

"It is quite clear that this will prove to be a costly mistake,"

noted Jarvis.   1 mark

END OF PRACTICE TEST PAPER 5

ENGLISH GRAMMAR, PUNCTUATION & SPELLING

PRACTICE TEST 6

FIRST NAME: _____

MIDDLE NAME: _____

LAST NAME: _____

DATE OF BIRTH: _____

SCHOOL NAME: _____

TOTAL SCORE: _____ / 50

1 Draw a line to connect each word to the correct **suffix** so that it makes an **adjective**.

Word

| civil |
| energy |
| wonder |

Suffix

| ous |
| ized |
| etic |

1 mark

2 Use the **conjunctions** from the box below to complete the following sentence. You may use each conjunction only **once**.

| though   whenever   now |

_____ the exam is over, you may leave _____ you are ready,

_____ you must hand in your answers first.

1 mark

3 Draw a circle around the **object** in the following sentence.

Last   week,   in   the   park,   my   friend   and   I   lost   our   favourite   football.

1 mark

4 Draw a line to connect each sentence to the correct **determiner**. You may use each determiner only **once**.

Sentence

| The restaurant had _____ kinds of drinks. |
| Eve said she didn't want _____ fruit juice. |
| She had _____ iced tea instead. |

Determiner

| some |
| all |
| any |

1 mark

5 Identify the option that must end with a **full stop**.

Tick one.

Won't the swimming team be participating ☐

Mary begged to go swimming ☐

What an amazing swimmer Carlos is ☐

She can't swim, can she ☐

1 mark

6 Show which sentence uses the **semi-colon** correctly.

Tick one.

Some people wear uniforms to work; such as doctors and nurses, other people, such as teachers and journalists, do not. ☐

Some people wear uniforms to work such as doctors and nurses, other people; such as teachers and journalists, do not. ☐

Some people wear uniforms to work, such as doctors and nurses, other people, such as teachers and journalists; do not. ☐

Some people wear uniforms to work, such as doctors and nurses; other people, such as teachers and journalists, do not. ☐

1 mark

7 Use an appropriate **adjective** to complete the following sentence.

The new exhibition is meant to be _____.

1 mark

8 Tick two boxes to identify where the missing **apostrophes** should go in the following sentence.

☐ ☐   ☐ ☐

The train to Leeds is late: its drivers been delayed by problems with his cars engine. 1 mark

9 Put **one** comma in the correct place in the following sentence.

Just   after   the   heavy   thunderstorm   ended   a   rainbow   appeared.

1 mark

10 Tick one box in each row to show whether the sentence is in the **present progressive** or the **past progressive**.

SENTENCE	Present progressive	Past progressive
Surprisingly, Sue is really enjoying studying science at the moment.		
She was not looking forward to learning about insects.		
However, she is finding it all very interesting, especially the bits about butterflies!		

1 mark

11 Use the correct **pronouns** to replace the underlined words in each of the following sentences.

Last Saturday, Jason and Tilly visited Josh — an old friend of Jason's and Tilly's.

In the afternoon, Josh helped Jason and Tilly build a snowman.

1 mark

12 Show which sentence uses the **hyphen** correctly.

Tick one.

She's a well-meaning but accident-prone girl. ☐

She's a well-meaning-but-accident-prone girl. ☐

She's a well-meaning-but accident prone girl. ☐

She's a well meaning-but-accident prone girl. ☐

1 mark

13 Identify the sentence that shows Omar is **most likely** to help.

Tick one.

Omar said he could help me. ☐

Omar said he might help me. ☐

Omar said he would help me. ☐

Omar said he may help me. ☐

1 mark

14 Draw a line to connect each sentence to its correct **function**. You may use each function only once.

Sentence

All the guests should bring presents with them, shouldn't they

All the guests are expected to bring a present with them

What amazing presents all the guests have brought with them

If you are a guest, bring at least one present with you

Function

statement

command

question

exclamation

1 mark

15 Identify the sentence which is written in **Standard** English.

Tick one.

I don't want nobody to help me. ☐

Jill doesn't want either of them books. ☐

We don't never want to see that film again. ☐

Neither of those dresses fits me anymore. ☐

1 mark

16 (a) Identify the punctuation marks on either side of the words <u>which is a fake according to some people</u> in the following sentence.

That painting — which is a fake according to some people — is currently on display.

_____

1 mark

(b) Name a **different** punctuation mark which could be used correctly in the same places.

_____

1 mark

17 Using the boxes given, write the **expanded forms** of the underlined words in each of the following sentences.

The coach said <u>she's</u> been watching the team and thinks <u>they'll</u> do very well.

| |
| |

Pamela and Rana <u>should've</u> arrived by now.

| |

1 mark

18 Your teacher is helping you to correct the punctuation of the sentence in the following box. Which **two** pieces of advice are you given?

| "My name is Hercules said the young elf. |

Tick two.

There should be a full stop after the word 'Hercules'. ☐

There should be inverted commas before the word 'said'. ☐

The word 'elf' should have a capital letter. ☐

There should be a comma after the word 'Hercules'. ☐

There should be a comma after the word 'young'. ☐

1 mark

19 Show which sentence uses **capital letters** correctly.

Tick one.

The Great Fire of London started in Pudding Lane. ☐

The great Fire of London started in Pudding Lane. ☐

The great fire of London started in Pudding Lane. ☐

The Great Fire of London started in Pudding lane. ☐

1 mark

20 Insert a **colon** in the correct place in the following sentence.

Crosswords are great fun they are a source of entertainment and

relaxation at the same time.

1 mark

21 Show the meaning of the root <u>corp</u> in the word family below.

corporeal   corporation   incorporate

Tick one.

company ☐

make ☐

join ☐

body ☐

1 mark

22 In the passage below, circle the word that contains an **apostrophe** for **possession**.

I'm amazed at these designer shoes as they're so impractical. They've

got extremely high heels and the shoes' price tags are so ridiculous

that I'd only wear them once a year — if at all.

1 mark

23 Tick one box in each row to show if the **commas** have been used correctly in the sentence.

SENTENCE	Commas used correctly	Commas used incorrectly
Many people's devices, including desktops and laptops, use Windows.		
Oscar likes having hot drinks while, his brother, prefers cold ones.		
Before you leave make sure, you've got all your belongings with you.		
You can have vanilla ice cream, chocolate cake, caramel fudge, or fresh fruit for dessert.		

1 mark

24 In the sentence below, circle all the **prepositions**.

She left her boots beside the wardrobe and put her jacket on a

hanger before she found her slippers.

1 mark

25 Rearrange the words in the following statement to turn it into a question. Use the given words only. Make sure you punctuate your answer correctly.

Statement: Mira and Jessie were frightened by the noise.

Question: _____

1 mark

26 In the sentence below, circle the two words that show the **tense**.

Today, sailors have radar to guide them; in the past, however, they

used the stars at night.

1 mark

27 In each of the following sentences, underline the **relative clause**.

Roger, who's visiting us at the moment, is sleeping in our living room.

Tim and Sue have agreed to meet in the park which is not far from here.

The local bookshop that I go to the most is called 'Mrs Bee's Books'. ‾1 mark

28 Circle the **conjunction** in each of the following sentences.

One day, whilst he was exploring a remote part of the Amazon rainforest,

Dr Galbraith stumbled across an ancient temple.

After lunch, Kamal felt rather sleepy, so he decided to take a short nap. ‾1 mark

29 In each of the following, show whether the underlined clause is a **main clause** or a **subordinate clause** by ticking one box.

SENTENCE	Main clause	Subordinate clause
<u>You should visit the Tower of London</u> which is where the Crown Jewels are kept.		
Don't wait for us <u>as we may be back late tonight</u>.		
The programme <u>that was being broadcast that evening</u> was rather boring.		

1 mark

30 (a) Add a **comma** to the following sentence to make it clear that **only** the sharks and the dolphins swam off.

After they'd eaten the fish the sharks and the dolphins swam off. ‾1 mark

(b) Add **commas** to the following sentence to make it clear that **all** the creatures swam off.

After they'd eaten the fish the sharks and the dolphins swam off. ‾1 mark

31 How do the different **prefixes** change the meanings of the two following sentences?

This argument must be <u>improved</u>.

This means that the argument must be _____

_____

_____

This argument must be <u>disproved</u>.

This means that the argument must be _____

_____

_____ 1 mark

32 Circle the two **conjunctions** in the following sentence.

Imagine   Mandy's   surprise   when   her   parents   bought   her   the   game

console   that   she'd   wanted   to   have   for   over   a   year!   1 mark

33 Use the correct **possessive pronoun** to replace the underlined word or words in each of the following sentences.

This sock belongs to <u>you</u>. It is _____.

The bakery is owned by <u>Mr and Mrs Mason</u>. It is _____.

Those tennis rackets belong to <u>my brother and me</u>. They are _____.   1 mark

34 (a) Explain the meaning of the word **antonym**.

_____

_____ 1 mark

(b) Write one word that is an **antonym** of the word <u>placid</u>.

_____ 1 mark

35 Rewrite the verbs in the boxes below using the **present progressive tense** to complete the following sentences.

Oliver _____ the cream while Ronan and Hugh _____ the cake tin.

whip

grease

The teacher _____ the situation.

reassess

1 mark

36 Using **adjectives** derived from the nouns in brackets, complete the following passage. One has been done for you.

Sadly, both the judge and the jury were _____**prejudiced**_____ [prejudice]. This meant

that the accused man received a trial that was neither _____ [justice] nor

_____ [law].

1 mark

37 Choose the option that completes the following sentence correctly.

My sister's science teacher _____ I've never met used to work at a famous university.

Tick one.

whom ☐

who ☐

whose ☐

which ☐

1 mark

38 Use the word <u>aim</u> as a **verb** in a sentence of your own. Do not change the word. Make sure you punctuate your sentence correctly.

_____

1 mark

Use the word <u>aim</u> as a **noun** in a sentence of your own. Do not change the word. Make sure you punctuate your sentence correctly.

_____

1 mark

39 In the following sentence, underline the **main clause**.

Rob,   whose   father   was   a   very   famous   ornithologist,   artist   and   chef,

is   my   neighbour.

1 mark

40 Tick one box in each row to show if the sentence is written in the **active voice** or in the **passive voice**.

SENTENCE	Active voice	Passive voice
Last week, our electricity supply was cut off.		
This was caused by a very bad storm.		
The power was restored after a few hours.		

1 mark

41 Rewrite the following sentence so that it is written in the **passive voice**. Make sure you punctuate your sentence correctly.

Last year's champions beat us in the final.

_____

1 mark

42 Identify the two **adjectives** in the sentence below by drawing a circle around each one.

The   ogre   cried   long   and   hard   because   he   was   friendless

and   lonely.

1 mark

43 Select the option which shows how the underlined words in the following sentence are used.

<u>On the distant horizon</u>, the travellers saw what appeared to be an oasis.

Tick one.

a subordinate clause   ☐

a preposition phrase   ☐

a main clause   ☐

a relative clause   ☐

1 mark

44 Select the verb that completes the sentence in the **subjunctive form**.

If I _____ you, I'd have the fish and chips.

Tick one.

was   ☐

being   ☐

am   ☐

were   ☐

1 mark

45 Identify the function of the following sentence.

What well-behaved children they are

Tick one.

a question ☐

a statement ☐

an exclamation ☐

a command ☐

1 mark

46 Show which sentence is written in the **present perfect simple form**.

Tick one.

She has been writing a poem for Mother's Day. ☐

Julia and Farida have something they want to say. ☐

They'd been there since 5 o'clock. ☐

I have warned you of the consequences. ☐

1 mark

END OF PRACTICE TEST PAPER 6

ENGLISH GRAMMAR, PUNCTUATION & SPELLING

PRACTICE TEST 7

First name: _____

Middle name: _____

Last name: _____

Date of birth: _____

School name: _____

Total score: _____ / 50

1 Identify the sentence that must end with an **exclamation mark**.

Tick one.

Have our team won the cup ☐

They said they had won the cup ☐

How wonderful that we've won the cup ☐

I was glad the team had won the cup ☐

1 mark

2 Insert a **colon** in the correct place in the following sentence.

You will need several things for the school camping trip next week sleeping

bags, a few cooking utensils, waterproof jackets, Wellington boots and

several warm sweaters.

1 mark

3 Identify the sentence that uses **capital letters** correctly.

Tick one.

As he loves english history, Ed's bought a book about the Stuarts. ☐

As he loves English History, Ed's bought a book about the stuarts. ☐

As he loves English history, Ed's bought a book about the stuarts. ☐

As he loves English history, Ed's bought a book about the Stuarts. ☐

1 mark

4 The **prefix** inter- can be used with the word stellar to make the word interstellar. What does the word **interstellar** mean?

Tick one.

between stars ☐

beyond stars ☐

below stars ☐

above stars ☐

1 mark

5 Identify the **verb form** that completes the sentence correctly.

Mr Brown has just announced he _____ in next year's election.

	Tick one.
hasn't run	☐
isn't running	☐
aren't running	☐
hadn't run	☐

1 mark

6 Complete the following sentences by circling the correct **verb form** in each underlined pair.

Sandy **doesn't / don't** know anything about this.

Like Kate and Jack, Bob **doesn't / don't** really enjoy barbecues.

If Eric **doesn't / don't** apologise, I'm never going to speak to him again.   1 mark

7 Select the option that completes the following sentence correctly.

_____ cooking and rushed outside to see what the matter was.

	Tick one.
Hearing a loud yell, Rupert stopped	☐
Hearing a, loud yell Rupert stopped	☐
Hearing a loud yell Rupert stopped,	☐
Hearing a loud, yell Rupert stopped	☐

1 mark

8 Identify the sentence that is correctly punctuated.

I feel really awful about the misunderstanding; however, I have no idea how it happened honestly, I don't. ☐

I feel really awful about the misunderstanding: however I have no idea how it happened — honestly I don't. ☐

I feel really awful about the misunderstanding; however, I have no idea how it happened — honestly, I don't. ☐

I feel really awful: about the misunderstanding, however, I have no idea how it happened; honestly I don't. ☐ $\overline{1\ mark}$

9 Identify the **word class** of the underlined word in the following sentence.

The job was <u>demanding</u>, but Joel was prepared to work extremely hard.

Tick one.

adverb ☐

preposition ☐

determiner ☐

adjective ☐ $\overline{1\ mark}$

10 Tick one box to identify the correct place for a **dash** in the following sentence.

Ella heaved a huge sigh of relief as she finally wrapped the last
☐ ☐

of her daughter's birthday presents she'd finished!
☐ ☐ $\overline{1\ mark}$

11 Identify the **word class** of the underlined words in the following sentence.

I <u>last</u> saw Carmen <u>just</u> after she got back from her summer holiday.

Tick one.

prepositions	☐
conjunctions	☐
adverbs	☐
determiners	☐

1 mark

12 Identify the sentence that is correctly punctuated.

Tick one.

The knight refused; all help he was determined to travel alone.	☐
The knight refused all help; he was determined to travel alone.	☐
The knight refused all help he was determined; to travel alone.	☐
The knight refused all help he was determined to travel; alone.	☐

1 mark

13 Identify the sentence that uses the word <u>flat</u> as an **adverb**.

Tick one.

I find <u>flat</u> shoes the most comfortable.	☐
These boxes fold <u>flat</u> for storage.	☐
Nina grew up in a small <u>flat</u> in a quiet Italian town.	☐
People used to believe the earth was <u>flat</u>.	☐

1 mark

14 Identify the sentence that is correctly punctuated.

Our trip and a very long trip — it was, too — took over 12 hours. ☐

Our trip — and a very long trip — it was, too took over 12 hours. ☐

Our trip — and a very long trip it was, too — took over 12 hours. ☐

Our trip — and a very long trip it was, too took — over 12 hours. ☐   1 mark

15 Identify the sentence that uses **capital letters** correctly.

Tick one.

What are the key characteristics of the African Elephant? ☐

"You're terribly naughty!" scolded auntie Mabel. ☐

One day, I'd like to travel to the Planet Mars. ☐

Kobo the Magician will not be performing this coming Friday. ☐   1 mark

16 Use an appropriate **subordinating conjunction** to complete the sentence below.

Vijay will be punished _____ his bad behaviour continues.   1 mark

17 Identify the sentence that is a **command**.

Tick one.

If you go swimming, remember to take your goggles ☐

Here are the rules that must be followed ☐

You will need to clean your shoes before you go out ☐

Could you hand me that saucepan ☐   1 mark

18 Show which sentence uses the word <u>down</u> as a **preposition**.

Tick one.

When you get to the top, make sure you don't look <u>down</u>. ☐

I can't believe Farida can <u>down</u> 4 litres of water a day! ☐

Jim was rather <u>down</u> yesterday; do you know why? ☐

Tears were streaming <u>down</u> the princess's face. ☐

1 mark

19 Insert **three commas** in the correct places in the following sentence.

My older cousin Stefan who lived in Glasgow before he moved to Durham with his parents when he was ten is a brilliant guitarist and an accomplished saxophonist.

1 mark

20 Use the correct **pronouns** to replace the underlined words in the following sentence.

Gina read the instructions on the box carefully; having read <u>the instructions</u> a second time, Gina threw <u>the box</u> away.

1 mark

21 Identify the sentence that is correctly punctuated.

Tick one.

The teacher asked, "Do any of you know who discovered gravity?". ☐

The teacher asked, "Do any of you know who discovered gravity?" ☐

The teacher asked "do any of you know who discovered gravity?" ☐

The teacher asked: "Do any of you know who discovered gravity"? ☐

1 mark

22 Identify the most **formal** sentence below.

Tick one.

I don't know how I will finish this work by tomorrow. ☐

We were informed that the work was needed by the next day. ☐

It is essential that the work be done by tomorrow. ☐

This work has to be finished by tomorrow. ☐

1 mark

23 Show which underlined group of words forms a **subordinate clause**.

Tick one.

Unless something changes, <u>this is not going to end well</u>. ☐

<u>My cousin Ivan</u> likes listening to rock music and jazz. ☐

A cat, <u>with very long whiskers</u>, was sitting on the wall. ☐

I think I would be very tired <u>if I were the headmaster</u>. ☐

1 mark

24 In the sentence below, circle the two words that are **antonyms**.

While the stubborn, bad-tempered elves refused to move another inch before they'd had something to eat, the woodland fairies were much more energetic and flexible.

1 mark

25 Tick one box in each row to show whether the apostrophe is used for **possession** or for a **contracted form**.

SENTENCE	Apostrophe used for possession	Apostrophe used for a contracted form
Tomorrow, we're having a party.		
Liam's coughing is worse today.		
The knight's armour was rusty.		
Paula's been to over twenty countries.		

1 mark

26 Show which sentence contains a **relative clause**.

Tick one.

Aisha read a lot of books while she was on holiday last summer. ☐

The Cornish cave which was used by smugglers has been flooded. ☐

"What is Ellie doing with that mop?" asked Dave. ☐

Jason's had that orange jumper for twenty years. ☐

1 mark

27 Show which sentence below is a **question**.

Tick one.

Jane asked me to help her ☐

Ask if you can help her ☐

She can't help us, can she ☐

Let's ask Jane for her help ☐

1 mark

28 Insert **capital letters** and **full stops** in the following passage so that it is correctly punctuated.

My brother speaks fluent french although he's never had lessons i have been studying it for five years and still find it difficult to speak the language my german, however, is much better than his

1 mark

29 Insert a **pair of brackets** in the correct place in the following sentence.

The tour guide told us that ancient Roman frescoes especially those which are to be found in the famous city of Pompeii are notable sources of information about ancient Roman painting.

1 mark

30 Rewrite the verbs in the boxes below using the correct **tense** to complete the sentences.

After he _____ Helen of Sparta, Paris took her to Troy: his home.

| to kidnap |

Currently, these thick walls _____ with the strength of our Wi-Fi.

| to interfere |

1 mark

31 Write a **command** which could be the first step in the directions you give your friend to get to your house. Make sure you punctuate your answer correctly.

_____

1 mark

32 In the following sentence, identify each of the clauses as either **main (M)** or **subordinate (S)**.

A priceless, medieval manuscript was found while the local library was being refurbished;

☐ ☐

it is now on display in the Town Hall.

☐

1 mark

33 In each of the following sentences, circle the **conjunction**.

Alice said she'd come to the meeting if she had time.

Many men before him had failed to find the treasure, yet the young shepherd

was convinced he would succeed.

During the match, the fans shouted whenever their team took a wicket.

1 mark

34 Show which two sentences contain a **preposition**.

Tick two.

The hunter moved cautiously as he neared the tiger. ☐

A Passage to India is a famous English novel. ☐

The words 'push' and 'pull' have opposite meanings. ☐

My brothers and I travelled together during the summer. ☐

1 mark

35 Identify the **subject** of the following sentence.

Last Sunday afternoon, a herd of cows escaped from a local farmer's field in Yorkshire.

Tick one.

Sunday afternoon ☐

Yorkshire ☐

herd of cows ☐

local farmer's field ☐

1 mark

36 Insert a **colon** and a **dash** in the correct places in the following sentence.

I watched a programme about a young maths genius a teenager from

a small Greek island I'd never heard of before it was remarkable! 1 mark

37 Circle the **relative pronoun** in the following sentence.

After he retired from professional football, Mr Johnson, whose daughter

was at school with my sister, became the manager of our local club. 1 mark

38 Rewrite the verbs in the boxes below using the **present perfect simple tense** to complete the following sentence.

Vicky _____ to write an account of our trip, but she

| to offer |

_____ this difficult as she _____ a headache for two days now.

| to find | | to have |

39 Insert a **pair of commas** in the correct place in the following sentence.

Mr   Robert   Davenport   is   a   keen   sailor   as   well   as   a   bit   of   an

amateur   comedian   who   rows   across   the   English   Channel   twice   each

year.

40 Identify the one **prefix** which can be added to all three of the following words to make their antonyms. Write your answer in the box.

classify
motivate
regulate

41 Circle the two words that are **synonyms** in the following passage.

The   contaminated   water   of   the   lake   had   a   peculiar   reddish   tinge.

It   also   had   a   malodorous   smell.   Although   attempts   at   disinfecting   it

had   been   made,   it   remained   polluted.

42 Circle the **possessive pronoun** in the following passage.

"I think that dress is pretty," Tina said to me. "However, yours is

more fashionable. I would like to buy one like it. Where did you

get it from?"

43 Identify which **punctuation mark** should be used in the place indicated by the arrow.

Eventually, after decades of war, the elves and the goblins made peace and settled their
differences nevertheless, suspicions remained on both sides.
↑

Tick one.

colon ☐

hyphen ☐

bracket ☐

semi-colon ☐

1 mark

44 Use a word formed from the root word <u>calm</u> to complete each of the following sentences.

Beth always behaves _____ during a crisis.

The giant _____ down once the mouse disappeared.

1 mark

45 Use a **verb** formed from the noun <u>embarrassment</u> to complete the following sentence.

"Stop that right now! You _____ me!" hissed Juliana.   1 mark

46 Insert **two hyphens** in the correct places in the following sentence.

Ali's   history   teacher   told   him   that   he'd   written   a   well   thought   out

essay   which   was   full   of   interesting   information   and   persuasive   arguments

about   the   English   Civil   War.

1 mark

47 Rewrite the following sentence in the **passive voice**. Make sure you punctuate your answer correctly.

Phil and Gina have caught the wrong bus by mistake.

_____

1 mark

48 Rewrite the verbs that are underlined in the following sentence so that they are in the **present perfect progressive** form.

While Mary <u>irons</u> her shirts, she <u>whistles</u> quietly to herself.

1 mark

49 Complete the following sentence using a **noun phrase** containing at least three words. Make sure you punctuate your answer correctly.

In honour of his bravery, the fireman was given a medal by _____

_____

1 mark

50 Circle the **adverb** in the following sentence.

Brimming   with   excitement,   Pip   was   wide   awake;   he   could   not   get   to   sleep.   1 mark

END OF PRACTICE TEST PAPER 7

ENGLISH GRAMMAR, PUNCTUATION & SPELLING

PRACTICE TEST 8

FIRST NAME: _____

MIDDLE NAME: _____

LAST NAME: _____

DATE OF BIRTH: _____

SCHOOL NAME: _____

TOTAL SCORE: _____ / 50

1 Draw a line to connect each word to the correct **suffix** so that it makes an **adjective**.

Word	Suffix
picture	ical
astronomy	ive
decision	esque

1 mark

2 Use the **conjunctions** from the box below to complete the following sentence. You may use each conjunction only **once**.

as	though	yet

_____ the performance had been short, _____ the audience

applauded loudly _____ it had been brilliant.

1 mark

3 Draw a circle around the **object** in the following sentence.

Tomorrow   evening,   after   dinner,   the   twins   are   planning   to   watch   the

match   at   a   friend's   house.

1 mark

4 Draw a line to connect each sentence to the correct **determiner**. You may use each determiner only **once**.

Sentence	Determiner
_____ books look interesting.	the
I think I'll buy _____ one about snakes.	these
They don't have _____ copies left.	many

1 mark

5 Identify the sentence that must end with an **exclamation mark**.

Tick one.

If you want anything, just ask me ☐

What did you ask me to do ☐

What a thing to ask of me ☐

Asking me to do something is never a good idea ☐

1 mark

6 Show which sentence uses the **colon** correctly.

Tick one.

Later, he realised the truth: right from the start, he had never wanted to study engineering. ☐

Later, he realised the truth right from the start he: had never wanted to study engineering. ☐

Later, he realised the truth, right from the start: he had never wanted to study engineering. ☐

Later, he realised: the truth right from the start he had never wanted to study engineering. ☐

1 mark

7 Use an appropriate **adverb** to complete the following sentence.

They arrived _____ for their appointment.

1 mark

8 Tick two boxes to identify where the missing **inverted commas** should go in the following sentence.

☐ ☐ ☐ ☐

Charles sheepishly admitted to his wife, I can't remember where I've parked the car!

1 mark

9 Put **one** colon in the correct place in the following sentence.

Near   the   hermit's   hut   was   a   river   that   eventually   flowed   into   a

lake   the   Waters   of   Forgetfulness   and   Peace.

1 mark

10 Tick one box in each row to show whether the sentence is in the **present perfect progressive** or the **past perfect progressive**.

SENTENCE	Present perfect progressive	Past perfect progressive
The orchestra has been rehearsing very hard for the concert next week.		
All of the members had been worrying that they wouldn't be ready.		
Consequently, they have been spending long hours perfecting their performance.		

1 mark

11 Use the correct **pronouns** to replace the underlined words in each of the following sentences.

Aunt Paige took <u>my cousin and me</u> to see a French film. After the film ended,

Aunt Paige, <u>my cousin and I</u> agreed that the film had been rather confusing.

1 mark

12 Show which sentence uses the **hyphen** correctly.

Tick one.

He was proud of his family's three hundred-year-old name.   ☐

He was proud of his family's three-hundred-year-old-name.   ☐

He was proud of his family's three-hundred year-old name.   ☐

He was proud of his family's three-hundred-year-old name.   ☐

1 mark

13 Identify the sentence that shows you are **least likely** to get the job.

Tick one.

As I'm highly qualified, I shall get the job. ☐

As I'm highly qualified, I may get the job. ☐

As I'm highly qualified, I will get the job. ☐

As I'm highly qualified, I must get the job. ☐

1 mark

14 Draw a line to connect each sentence to its correct **function**. You may use each function only **once**.

Sentence	Function

Sentence	Function
Once you've bought the tickets, make sure you give one to Jane	statement
How excited Jane will be when you give her her ticket	question
When the tickets have been bought, one must be given to Jane	exclamation
After you've bought the tickets, could you give one to Jane	command

1 mark

15 Identify the sentence which is written in **Non-Standard** English.

Tick one.

One of these solutions should've worked. ☐

Poppy was surprised to find that all the chores had been done. ☐

I realised I'd forgotten my phone charger at home. ☐

Una was given a canteen of cutlery as a wedding present. ☐

1 mark

16 (a) Identify the punctuation marks on either side of the words <u>as she always does when we've been out</u> in the following sentence.

Mum insisted (as she always does when we've been out) that we wash our hands.

_____

1 mark

(b) Name a **different** punctuation mark which could be used correctly in the same places.

_____

1 mark

17 Using the boxes given, write the **contracted forms** of the underlined words in the following sentences.

That <u>does not</u> look right; <u>you had</u> better check it.

Unfortunately, we <u>will not</u> be able to come next week.

1 mark

18 Your teacher is helping you to correct the punctuation of the sentence in the following box. Which **two** pieces of advice are you given?

Stop, "thief" cried the angry shopkeeper.

Tick two.

There should be an exclamation mark after the word 'thief'. ☐

There should be a comma after the word 'cried'. ☐

There should be inverted commas after the word 'shopkeeper'. ☐

The sentence should end with an exclamation mark, not a full stop. ☐

There should be inverted commas before the word 'Stop', not 'thief'. ☐

1 mark

19 Show which sentence uses **capital letters** correctly.

Tick one.

Queen Elizabeth I succeeded her sister, queen Mary I, in 1558. ☐

Queen elizabeth I succeeded her sister, Queen Mary i, in 1558. ☐

Queen Elizabeth i succeeded her sister, Queen mary I, in 1558. ☐

Queen Elizabeth I succeeded her sister, Queen Mary I, in 1558. ☐

1 mark

20 Insert a **semi-colon** in the correct place in the following sentence.

My grandmother's favourite saying was 'Never a lender nor a borrower be' her least favourite saying of all was 'Every cloud has a silver lining'.

1 mark

21 Show the meaning of the root <u>termin</u> in the word family below.

terminal   in**termin**able   inde**termin**ate

Tick one.

boring ☐

boundary ☐

endless ☐

unclear ☐

1 mark

22 In the passage below, circle the word that contains an **apostrophe** for **contraction**.

According to my sister's friend, during the teachers' staff meeting, the naughty children's behaviour was discussed. As a result, the parents have been called in to see the headmaster; we're all wondering what will happen next!

1 mark

23 Tick one box in each row to show if the **semi-colon** has been used correctly in the sentence.

SENTENCE	Semi-colon used correctly	Semi-colon used incorrectly
The Italian dish contained; oregano; basil; and chilli flakes.		
Surprised to see me, Max asked; "How did you get here?"		
The name of the band was quite bizarre; Milly's Mushroom Marshmallows.		
There was only one word I could think of to describe it; catastrophic.		

1 mark

24 In the sentence below, circle all the **prepositions**.

During their summer holidays last year, while they were on a camping

trip, Mary, Thelma and Louise discovered some ancient Roman coins

buried beneath a large rock.

1 mark

25 Rearrange the words in the following statement to turn it into a question. Use the given words only. Make sure you punctuate your answer correctly.

Statement: Otto has been studying for three hours.

Question: _____

1 mark

26 In the sentence below, circle the two words that show the **tenses**.

Once upon a time, robots were pure science fiction; today, however,

they perform many tasks.

1 mark

27 In each of the following sentences, underline the **subordinate clause**.

"Unless someone comes to my rescue, I'm doomed," said the prince.

Tomorrow morning, if you wake up early enough, you will hear the birds sing.

Mr Singh is learning to speak Japanese even though it is very difficult.

1 mark

28 Circle the **conjunction** in each of the following sentences.

Irritatingly, it has started snowing, so we've decided to stay indoors.

"You should have something to eat before you go to school," Kelly's

mum advised her.

1 mark

29 In each of the following, show whether the underlined clause is a **main clause** or a **subordinate clause** by ticking one box.

SENTENCE	Main clause	Subordinate clause
<u>After he had decided to grow vegetables in his garden</u>, Felix planted lots of seeds.		
The tiny island was hit by a hurricane <u>which caused an immense amount of damage</u>.		
Whatever you may think at the moment, <u>I'm right</u>.		

1 mark

30 (a) Add a **comma** to the following sentence to make it clear that **only** Betty and Shelly came to the party.

As they'd promised Alex Betty and Shelly came to the party.

1 mark

(b) Add **commas** to the following sentence to make it clear that **all** three children came to the party.

As they'd promised Alex Betty and Shelly came to the party.

1 mark

31 How do the different **prefixes** change the meanings of the two following sentences?

This civilization <u>antedates</u> the ancient Greeks.

This means that this civilization _____

_____

_____

This civilization <u>postdates</u> the ancient Greeks.

This means that this civilization _____

_____

_____

1 mark

32 Circle the two **conjunctions** in the following sentence.

Raj   neither   enjoyed   studying   poetry   nor   did   he   like   novels;   his

interests   lay   firmly   in   the   sciences.   1 mark

33 Use the correct **possessive pronoun** to replace the underlined word or words in each of the following sentences.

Those pairs of shoes belong to <u>Stuart and Bart</u>. Those shoes are _____.

That cap doesn't belong to <u>me</u>. That cap is not _____.

The binoculars might belong to <u>Khaled</u>. The binoculars might be _____.   1 mark

34 (a) Explain the meaning of the word **synonym**.

_____

_____

1 mark

(b) Write one word that is a **synonym** of the word <u>overstatement</u>.

_____

1 mark

35 Rewrite the verbs in the boxes below using the **present perfect progressive tense** to complete the following sentences.

Helen _____ a great deal as she _____ from a nasty cold.

| cough |
| suffer |

We _____ to sell the antique table we inherited.

| plan |

1 mark

36 Using **adverbs** derived from the nouns in brackets, complete the following passage. One has been done for you.

The knight replied _____**angrily**_____ [anger] to the lord's accusation. He was not,

said the knight _____ [indignation], a coward. Nor, continued the knight

_____ [fury], was he a traitor to his king.

1 mark

37 Choose the option that completes the following sentence correctly.

The person _____ mess this is had better clean it up right now.

Tick one.

who's ☐

whom ☐

who'd ☐

whose ☐

1 mark

38 Use the word <u>contract</u> as a **verb** in a sentence of your own. Do not change the word. Make sure you punctuate your sentence correctly.

_____

1 mark

Use the word <u>contract</u> as a **noun** in a sentence of your own. Do not change the word. Make sure you punctuate your sentence correctly.

_____

1 mark

39 In the following sentence, underline the **relative clause**.

Crystal   Palace   was   an   impressive   building   that   was   designed   by   Joseph

Paxton   and   Owen   Jones   in   the   nineteenth   century.

1 mark

40 Tick one box in each row to show if the sentence is written in the **active voice** or in the **passive voice**.

SENTENCE	Active voice	Passive voice
Annoyingly, the concert was cancelled at the last minute.		
Everyone who had bought a ticket was extremely cross.		
None of us know whether we will receive refunds from the organisers.		

1 mark

41 Rewrite the following sentence so that it is written in the **active voice**. Make sure you punctuate your sentence correctly.

While he was sunbathing, Elias was stung by a large bumblebee.

_____

1 mark

42 Identify the two **adverbs** in the sentence below by drawing a circle around each one.

"I won't go to that cheap restaurant again," whined the spoilt child tiresomely.

1 mark

43 Select the option which shows how the underlined words in the following sentence are used.

<u>Three days ago</u>, when my new phone finally arrived, it was broken.

Tick one.

as a preposition phrase ☐

as a fronted adverbial ☐

as a relative clause ☐

as a subordinate clause ☐

1 mark

44 Select the verb that completes the sentence in the **subjunctive form**.

It is crucial she _____ at the meeting next Tuesday.

Tick one.

be ☐

is ☐

were ☐

are ☐

1 mark

45 Identify the function of the following sentence.

She decided to buy that lampshade, didn't she

Tick one.

an exclamation ☐

a statement ☐

a question ☐

a command ☐

1 mark

46 Show which sentence is written in the **present progressive form**.

Tick one.

Reading a biography of Mo Farah was how I spent my weekend. ☐

According to her teachers at school, Ola is doing extremely well. ☐

The singing children danced around the room. ☐

The two political parties have been arguing about this for years. ☐

1 mark

END OF PRACTICE TEST PAPER 8

Practice Test Papers 1, 2, 3, 4, 5, 6, 7 & 8

ANSWERS & MARKING GUIDELINES

Notes to Using the Answers & Marking Guidelines

Before using the Answers, please note the following:

MARKS

- After the correct answer to each question is given, the marking guidelines indicate **how many marks** each answer is worth.
- Half marks **may not be awarded** under any circumstances.

MULTIPLE ANSWERS

- When a question requires **more than one answer**, **ALL** the student's given **responses must be correct** for their answer to be regarded as right. For example, if the correct answers to a question are the words *his* and *him*, the student must provide both correct words.
- When a question can be **correctly answered in more than one way**, this is noted in this section and an **example** of at least **one possible correct** answer is given.

ADDITIONAL MARKING GUIDANCE

- Where necessary, additional marking guidance has been supplied in italics, including, on occasion, student responses **which cannot be accepted**.

ANSWERS TO 'TICK BOX' QUESTIONS

- Where the student has to show their chosen answer by ticking at least one box, this section gives the correct answer(s), followed by which box(es) should be ticked: *1st box, 2nd box, 3rd box, etc.*
  - For sets of vertical boxes, the topmost box is the 1st box, and so on.
  - For sets of horizontal boxes, the leftmost box is the 1st box, and so on.

(1) How did you do that **(2ND BOX)**
Award 1 MARK for the correct answer.

(2) power → less; child → hood; comfort → able; amuse → ment
Award 1 MARK for ALL 4 correct answers.

(3) Don't scare... → command;
Don't forget... → command;
Don't you ever... → question;
Don't go near... → command
Award 1 MARK for ALL 4 correct answers.

(4) Katy was late for school **again,** so she began to run.
Award 1 MARK for the correctly placed COMMA.

(5) dis → appoint; mis → take; sub → marine; in → secure
Award 1 MARK for ALL 4 correct answers.

(6) Make sure you take an umbrella **(4TH BOX)**
Award 1 MARK for the correct answer.

(7) I; were; likes
Award 1 MARK for ALL 3 correct answers.

(8) *Answers will differ, but MUST all be CORRECTLY SPELT & WRITTEN IN LOWER CASE. Examples:*
• *The film <u>which</u> I watched yesterday was...*
• *The film <u>that</u> I watched yesterday was...*
Award 1 MARK for an appropriate RELATIVE PRONOUN that has been correctly inserted.

(9) The mayor is going to <u>present</u> the prizes. **(4TH BOX)**
Award 1 MARK for the correct answer.

(10) Jane wanted to play **tennis;** her brother preferred to have a game of squash.
Award 1 MARK for the correctly placed SEMI-COLON.

(11) The orang-utan **(**one of the great apes**)** is an endangered species.
Award 1 MARK for the correctly placed PAIR OF BRACKETS.

(12) between **(2ND BOX)**
Award 1 MARK for the correct answer.

(13) Some tourists — probably from Germany — asked me the way to the station. **(2ND BOX)**
Award 1 MARK for the correct answer.

(14) abandoned **(3RD BOX)**
Award 1 MARK for the correct answer.

(15) Would you care for another cup of tea? **(1ST BOX)**
Award 1 MARK for the correct answer.

(16) 4TH BOX
*The correct place for the missing hyphen is as follows: Bernie had some carrot sticks, cherry tomatoes, a banana and a **sugar-free** drink for lunch.*
Award 1 MARK for the correct answer.

(17) a preposition **(3RD BOX)**
Award 1 MARK for the correct answer.

(18) courageous; valiant
Award 1 MARK for BOTH correct answers.

(19) main clause
Award 1 MARK for a correct answer.
ALSO ACCEPT answers that use an abbreviation that makes the intention clear. Example:
• *main*
DO NOT ASSESS punctuation or spelling here.

(20) Nobody could find Jason — he was hiding in the garden.
Award 1 MARK for the correctly placed DASH.

(21) a co-ordinating conjunction **(1ST BOX)**
Award 1 MARK for the correct answer.

(22) Aunt May refuses to go **camping:** she is afraid of being bitten or stung by insects or creepy crawlies.
Award 1 MARK for the correctly placed COLON.

(23) Gerald enjoys **swimming,** playing **basketball,** rock **climbing,** reading detective novels and making models.
Award 1 MARK for ALL 3 correctly placed COMMAS.

(24) When Patrick said he had finished his homework, his mother looked surprised. **(4TH BOX)**
Award 1 MARK for the correct answer.

(25) I will call you on our return.
Award 1 MARK for the correct answer.

(26) remain
Award 1 MARK for the correct answer.

(27) <u>We</u> → S (subject); <u>cake</u> → O (object); <u>Giles</u> → S (subject); <u>it</u> → O (object)
Award 1 MARK for ALL 4 correct answers.

(28) ...Susie <u>goes</u> to... → went;
...always <u>swims</u> ten... → swam
Award 1 MARK for BOTH correct answers.
DO NOT ACCEPT any misspellings of the verb forms.

(29) Danny's leg is broken now. **(1ST BOX)**
Award 1 MARK for the correct answer.

(30) exhausted; steep; unwell
Award 1 MARK for ALL 3 correct answers.

(31) Harry asked hopefully, "Is there anything for supper?" **(2ND BOX)**
Award 1 MARK for the correct answer.

(32) The elves were quite peculiar. **(4TH BOX)**
Award 1 MARK for the correct answer.

(33) conjunction OR conjunctions OR subordinating conjunctions
Award 1 MARK for a correct answer.
DO NOT ASSESS punctuation or spelling here.

(34) *Answers will differ and may refer to either or both of the sentences. Examples:*
- *In the first sentence, Jan's aunt loves two things.*
- *The second sentence means that Jan's aunt loves three things.*
- *In sentence (i) the two things Jan's aunt loves are walking her dog and reading, but in sentence (ii) the three things Jan's aunt loves are walking, her dog and reading.*

Award 1 MARK for an answer that shows a correct understanding that THERE ARE 3 NAMED ACTIVITIES IN THE 2ND SENTENCE.
DO NOT ACCEPT general answers. Example:
- *It's a list.*

DO NOT ASSESS punctuation or spelling here.

(35) outside the cinema
Award 1 MARK for the correct answer.

(36) *Answers will differ, but MUST all be a GRAMMATICALLY CORRECT RELATIVE CLAUSE. Examples:*
- *The house, which was deserted, was extremely old.*
- *The house, that stood on the corner, was extremely old.*

Award 1 MARK for a correct answer.
DO NOT ACCEPT answers which are grammatically incorrect. Example:
- *The house, what was owned by Mr Smith, was extremely old.*

(37) *Answers will differ and may refer to either or both of the sentences. Examples:*
- *In the first sentence, he drove home first, then he began to complain.*
- *The second sentence means he began to complain at the same time he was driving home.*
- *In sentence (i) it tells us what he did after he drove home, but in sentence (ii) it tells us what he did when he was driving home.*

Award 1 MARK for an answer that shows a correct understanding that THE CONJUNCTION CHANGES THE CHRONOLOGICAL RELATIONSHIP BETWEEN THE ACTIONS.
DO NOT ACCEPT general answers. Example:
- *It changes when he did it.*

DO NOT ASSESS punctuation or spelling here.

(38) should
Award 1 MARK for the correct answer.

(39) *Answers will differ, but MUST all be CORRECTLY PUNCTUATED SENTENCES that CORRECTLY USE THE PASSIVE VOICE. Examples:*
- *The winner of the competition was congratulated.*
- *The winner of the competition was congratulated by the headmaster.*

Award 1 MARK for a correct answer.
DO NOT ACCEPT misspellings of the verb forms or answers which change the verb or the tense.

(40) In the **autumn,** the trees...their **leaves,** making...work **hard;** they go...
Award 1 MARK for BOTH the correctly placed COMMAS and SEMI-COLON.

(41) pianist; performance; night
Award 1 MARK for ALL 3 correct answers.

(42) They were encouraged by their coach. **(3RD BOX)**
Award 1 MARK for the correct answer.

(43) should have → should've
Award 1 MARK for the correct answer.
DO NOT ACCEPT misspellings.

(44) historian; historical
Award 1 MARK for BOTH correct answers.
DO NOT ACCEPT misspellings or words written in upper case.

(45) noun phrase(s)
Award 1 MARK for a correct answer.
ALSO ACCEPT expanded / extended noun phrase OR grammatical function (i.e. subject).
DO NOT ASSESS punctuation or spelling here.

(46) **in december,** **mr mantovani** is planning to go to **manchester** to do his **christmas** shopping.
Award 1 MARK for ALL 6 correct answers.

(47) much; two; the
Award 1 MARK for ALL 3 correct answers.

(48) The **children's** books were on the shelves.
Award 1 MARK for the correctly placed APOSTROPHE.

(49) at; of; opposite
Award 1 MARK for ALL 3 correct answers.

(50) and
Award 1 MARK for the correct answer.

(1) As Jeff was not answering his **phone,** I decided not to buy him a ticket.
Award 1 MARK for the correctly inserted COMMA.

(2) How regularly does this happen **(3RD BOX)**
Award 1 MARK for the correct answer.

(3) to fail to work **(1ST BOX)**
Award 1 MARK for the correct answer.

(4) Iguanas are insectivorous... → statement;
Do you know... → question;
If you don't... → command;
These lizards live... → statement
Award 1 MARK for ALL 4 correct answers.

(5) Our Uncle Phillip loves **rowing, boats,** fishing and rivers.
Award 1 MARK for BOTH correctly inserted COMMAS.

(6) loudly **(1ST BOX)**
Award 1 MARK for the correct answer.

(7) I've put the brown **briefcase,** that smells a bit **musty,** in the attic.
Award 1 MARK for the correctly inserted PAIR OF COMMAS.

(8) Three weeks ago, we had no idea this would happen. **(2ND BOX)**
Award 1 MARK for the correct answer.

(9) clash **(4TH BOX)**
Award 1 MARK for the correct answer.

(10) Take the 38 bus to Olive Road. **(2ND BOX)**
Award 1 MARK for the correct answer.

(11) de → value; em → body; dis → regard; im → port
Award 1 MARK for ALL 4 correct answers.

(12) had stolen **(4TH BOX)**
Award 1 MARK for the correct answer.

(13) All the cold water in the fridge had been drunk. **(1ST BOX)**
Award 1 MARK for the correct answer.

(14) Abi enjoys drawing mandalas — their intricate designs are very satisfying. **(2ND BOX)**
Award 1 MARK for the correct answer.

(15) an adverbial **(4TH BOX)**
Award 1 MARK for the correct answer.

(16) How did you get here so quickly **(1ST BOX)**
Award 1 MARK for the correct answer.

(17) The miser loved but two **things:** his money and the vault that kept it safe.
Award 1 MARK for the correctly placed COLON.

(18) I'm sorry I can't stop; I'm in a terrible <u>hurry</u>. **(3RD BOX)**
Award 1 MARK for the correct answer.

(19) Suddenly, the temperature dropped rapidly and our teeth began to chatter. **(4TH BOX)**
Award 1 MARK for the correct answer.

(20) *Answers will differ and may refer to either or both of the sentences. Examples:*
- *In the first sentence, they definitely go scuba diving in Belize.*
- *In the second sentence, it means perhaps they will go scuba diving in Belize.*
- *In sentence (a) Chris and Omar certainly go scuba diving in Belize, but in sentence (b) they may go scuba diving in Belize.*

Award 1 MARK for an answer that CORRECTLY shows that the modal verb 'COULD' INDICATES UNCERTAINTY OR POSSIBILITY.
DO NOT ASSESS punctuation or spelling here.

(21) preposition **(2ND BOX)**
Award 1 MARK for the correct answer.

(22) *Answers will differ, but MUST all be CORRECTLY SPELT. Example:*
- *They learnt about dolphins <u>when</u> they were at the aquarium.*

Award 1 MARK for an appropriate SUBORDINATING CONJUNCTION that has been correctly inserted.

(23) removal *OR* removing
Award 1 MARK for a correct answer.
DO NOT ACCEPT any misspellings.

(24) ...aunt, <u>my aunt</u> always... → she;
...that <u>my aunt and I</u> do... → we;
...cook for <u>my aunt</u> for a... → her
Award 1 MARK for ALL 3 correctly spelt PRONOUNS.

(25) The residents ought to be consulted before a decision is made. **(3RD BOX)**
Award 1 MARK for the correct answer.

(26) *Answers will differ, but MUST all use CORRECT QUESTION PUNCTUATION. Examples:*
- *Where is the meeting being held?*
- *"Where is the meeting being held?"*

Award 1 MARK for a correct answer.
DO NOT ACCEPT answers in which the question is contained in a sentence. Example: Barry asked, "Where is the meeting being held?"

(27) a dangerous criminal *OR* criminal
Award 1 MARK for a correct answer.

(28) dash *OR* dashes *OR* (a) pair of dashes *OR* brackets *OR* (a) pair of brackets
Award 1 MARK for a correct answer.
DO NOT ASSESS punctuation or spelling here.

(29) proud; amazing; friends
Award 1 MARK for ALL 3 correctly identified WORDS.

(30) The firecrackers' explosions... → plural;
That writer's horror... → singular;
...our class's favourite... → singular
Award 1 MARK for ALL 3 correct answers.

(31) ...thinks fast → adverb;
...fast thinker → adjective
Award 1 MARK for BOTH correct answers.
DO NOT ASSESS punctuation or spelling here.

(32) The manager insisted Tim be fired. **(4TH BOX)**
Award 1 MARK for the correct answer.

(33) In; for; in; without
Award 1 MARK for ALL 4 correct answers.

(34) Helena's husband was an incredibly **sociable, good-looking** university lecturer.
Award 1 MARK for BOTH the correctly placed COMMA and HYPHEN.

(35) *Answers will differ and may refer to either or both of the sentences. Examples:*
- *In the first sentence, there is only one student.*
- *The second sentence means there is more than one student.*
- *In the second sentence, it shows plural possession.*
- *In sentence (i) there is one student, but in sentence (ii) there is more than one student.*
Award 1 MARK for an answer that shows a correct understanding of the PLURAL POSSESSIVE APOSTROPHE.
DO NOT ASSESS punctuation or spelling here.

(36) Louis Pasteur, a French scientist, is regarded as one of the 3 founders of bacteriology. **(2ND BOX)**
I find some fruit — particularly lychees, mangosteens and rambutans — rather odd. **(3RD BOX)**
Award 1 MARK for BOTH correct answers.

(37) where they could hide their loot;
which has nine sides;
whose name is Squiggly
Award 1 MARK for ALL 3 correct answers.

(38) ...family go to... → went;
...always have a... → had
Award 1 MARK for BOTH correct answers.
DO NOT ACCEPT any misspellings of the verb forms.

(39) (a) relative clause *OR* (a) subordinate clause
Award 1 MARK for a correct answer.
DO NOT ASSESS punctuation or spelling here.

(40) The results should... → passive;
Troops are being... → passive;
The temperature has... → active
Award 1 MARK for ALL 3 correct answers.

(41) *Answers will differ, but MUST all be an APPROPRIATE, GRAMMATICALLY CORRECT and CORRECTLY PUNCTUATED sentence in DIRECT SPEECH. Example:*
- *They asked, "Can we have some more juice?"*
Award 1 MARK for a correct answer.

(42) your
Award 1 MARK for the correct answer.

(43) *Answers will differ, but MUST all be a GRAMMATICALLY CORRECT and CORRECTLY PUNCTUATED sentence that uses an APPROPRIATE CO-ORDINATING CONJUNCTION. Example:*
- *She was very late for her appointment, yet she was walking slowly.*
Award 1 MARK for a correct answer.

(44) next Tuesday
Award 1 MARK for the correct answer.

(45) who
Award 1 MARK for the correct answer.

(46) distract → distracting;
simple → simplify
Award 1 MARK for BOTH correct answers.
DO NOT ACCEPT any misspellings.

(47) two of my favourite nursery rhyme characters used to be **old king cole** and **humpty dumpty**.
Award 1 MARK for ALL 6 correct answers.

(48) were; coming; switched; headed
Award 1 MARK for ALL 4 correct answers.

(49) experienced → are experiencing
Award 1 MARK for the correct answer.
DO NOT ACCEPT any misspellings of the verb forms.

(50) when we opened our front door
Award 1 MARK for the correct answer.

(1) fiction → al; expense → ive; courage → ous
Award 1 MARK for ALL 3 correct answers.

(2) I could quite happily eat a whole pizza **or** a huge plate of pasta, **for** I'm ravenous **as** I've not eaten since yesterday.
Award 1 MARK for ALL 3 correctly inserted CONJUNCTIONS.

(3) Mrs Mitcham *OR* poor Mrs Mitcham
Award 1 MARK for a correct answer.

(4) _____ cat killed the mouse. → neither;
Is there _____ explanation for this? → an;
_____ guess is as good as mine. → your
Award 1 MARK for ALL 3 correct answers.

(5) When the train will leave is not yet known **(4TH BOX)**
Award 1 MARK for the correct answer.

(6) Helen has had several pets: a cat, a gerbil, a hedgehog, a dog and a parrot. **(2ND BOX)**
Award 1 MARK for the correct answer.

(7) *Answers will differ, but MUST all be CORRECTLY SPELT. Example:*
• *Rihanna is <u>never</u> late for meetings.*
Award 1 MARK for the correct insertion of an appropriate ADVERB.

(8) **1ST BOX** & **2ND BOX**
The correct places for the missing inverted commas are as follows: "Are you all going swimming?" Molly asked.
Award 1 MARK for BOTH correct answers.

(9) Quickly and **quietly,** the thief moved around the empty house.
Award 1 MARK for the correctly inserted COMMA.

(10) Anne has been... → present perfect;
She had worked... → past perfect;
She has seemed... → present perfect
Award 1 MARK for ALL 3 correct answers.

(11) ...that <u>John</u> had... → he;
...replacing <u>the old car</u> with... → it
Award 1 MARK for BOTH correct PRONOUNS.

(12) My seven-year-old brother is very naughty. **(1ST BOX)**
Award 1 MARK for the correct answer.

(13) It won't snow tomorrow. **(3RD BOX)**
Award 1 MARK for the correct answer.

(14) I want you... → statement;
Make sure that... → command;
When are you... → question;

How fantastically clean... → exclamation
Award 1 MARK for ALL 4 correct answers.

(15) They has bought her a wonderful birthday present. **(4TH BOX)**
Award 1 MARK for the correct answer.

(16a) brackets *OR* a pair of brackets
Award 1 MARK for a correct answer.

(16b) commas *OR* a pair of commas *OR* dashes *OR* a pair of dashes
Award 1 MARK for a correct answer.

(17) ...application <u>was not</u> accepted... → wasn't;
...so <u>they are</u> going... → they're;
<u>We have</u> got... → We've
Award 1 MARK for ALL 3 correct answers.
DO NOT ACCEPT the use of the pronoun 'We' without a capital letter in this instance (i.e. we've).

(18) There should be a question mark after the word 'station', not 'asked'. **(3RD BOX)**
There should be a full stop at the end of the sentence. **(5TH BOX)**
Award 1 MARK for BOTH correct answers.

(19) Last September, a group of us went to the Greek island of Crete. **(1ST BOX)**
Award 1 MARK for the correct answer.

(20) For years, the Browns never had much **money;** that all changed when they won the lottery.
Award 1 MARK for the correctly placed SEMI-COLON.

(21) throw **(4TH BOX)**
Award 1 MARK for the correct answer.

(22) they're
Award 1 MARK for the correct answer.

(23) For this recipe... → commas used incorrectly;
A large number... → commas used correctly;
Jonah has visited... → commas used incorrectly;
The laptop, which... → commas used correctly
Award 1 MARK for ALL 4 correct answers.

(24) against; under
Award 1 MARK for BOTH correct answers.

(25) Have the children eaten their sandwiches?
Award 1 MARK for the correct answer.

(26) have; lived
Award 1 MARK for BOTH correct answers.

(27) Linda went for a walk in the park;
we're going home;
Val broke his arm
Award 1 MARK for ALL 3 correct answers.

(28) although; once
Award 1 MARK for BOTH correct answers.

(29) <u>The enemy spy waited patiently</u>... → main clause;
...<u>as he did not want to be seen</u> → subordinate clause;
...<u>he crept inside</u> → main clause
Award 1 MARK for ALL 3 correct answers.

(30a) Once they'd met **Ed,** Hal and Raj went to the shops.
Award 1 MARK for the correctly placed COMMA.

(30b) Once they'd **met, Ed,** Hal and Raj went to the shops.
Award 1 MARK for BOTH correctly placed COMMAS.
DO NOT ACCEPT the use of a serial comma: Once they'd met, Ed, <u>Hal,</u> and Raj went to the shops.

(31) *Answers will differ, but must CORRECTLY explain the MEANINGS of the verbs 'REREAD' and 'MISREAD'. Examples:*
- *Kelly has <u>reread</u> the article. → This means that the article <u>has been read again</u>.*
- *Kelly has <u>misread</u> the article. → This means that the article <u>has not been understood correctly</u>.*
Award 1 MARK for BOTH correct EXPLANATIONS.

(32) on; outside
Award 1 MARK for BOTH correct answers.

(33) ...to <u>my uncle</u> → his;
...by <u>my brother and sister</u> → theirs;
...to <u>my mother</u> → hers
Award 1 MARK for ALL 3 correct answers.

(34a) *Answers will differ. Example:*
- *Synonyms are words that mean the same thing.*
Award 1 MARK for a correct DEFINITION.

(34b) *Answers will differ. Example:*
- *logical.*
Award 1 MARK for a correct SYNONYM.

(35) be → is; employ → employs; manufacture → manufactures
Award 1 MARK for ALL 3 correct answers.
DO NOT ACCEPT misspellings of any of the verb forms.

(36) trust → trustworthy; care → careful
Award 1 MARK for BOTH correct ADJECTIVES.
ALSO ACCEPT trust → trusted.
DO NOT ACCEPT misspellings of the adjectives.

(37) whose **(2ND BOX)**
Award 1 MARK for the correct answer.

(38) *Answers will differ for each part of this question.*
Award 1 MARK for a GRAMMATICALLY CORRECT and CORRECTLY
PUNCTUATED sentence that uses 'BREAK' as a VERB. Example:
- *I didn't mean to <u>break</u> your watch.*
DO NOT ACCEPT answers that change the given form of the verb. Example: I'm sorry I <u>broke</u> your watch.

Award 1 MARK for a GRAMMATICALLY CORRECT and CORRECTLY
PUNCTUATED sentence that uses 'BREAK' as a NOUN. Example:
- *The children played hopscotch during <u>break</u>.*
DO NOT ACCEPT answers that change the given form of the noun. Example: Luke takes far too many <u>breaks</u> at work.

(39) who was born a Spanish princess
Award 1 MARK for the FULL correct answer.

(40) A gate was... → passive voice;
Some of the animals... → active voice;
Luckily, they were... → passive voice
Award 1 MARK for ALL 3 correct answers.

(41) I was bitten by a large, poisonous snake.
Award 1 MARK for a CORRECTLY PUNCTUATED sentence in the PASSIVE VOICE.
ALSO ACCEPT I was bitten.

(42) clean; fresh
Award 1 MARK for BOTH correct answers.

(43) as a fronted adverbial **(4TH BOX)**
Award 1 MARK for the correct answer.

(44) be **(2ND BOX)**
Award 1 MARK for the correct answer.

(45) a command **(1ST BOX)**
Award 1 MARK for the correct answer.

(46) The angry cyclist was shouting at the careless driver.
(3RD BOX)
Award 1 MARK for the correct answer.

(1) When does the train depart **(1ST BOX)**
Award 1 MARK for the correct answer.

(2) were are **(4TH BOX)**
Award 1 MARK for the correct answer.

(3) ir → responsible; il → legal; sub → marine; inter → national; in → accurate
Award 1 MARK for ALL 5 correct answers.

(4) All around her, she could see a glistening blanket of snow. **(3RD BOX)**
Award 1 MARK for the correct answer.

(5) It was completed in the nineteenth century. **(2ND BOX)**
Award 1 MARK for the correct answer.

(6) They **were** waiting for the bus for ages.
It **was** half an hour late.
Award 1 MARK for BOTH correct answers.

(7) Ed <u>should have</u> arrived... → should've
Award 1 MARK for the correct answer.

(8) What a terrible defeat for the team **(4TH BOX)**
Award 1 MARK for the correct answer.

(9) Owing to the storm, people's houses were damaged.
(1ST BOX)
Award 1 MARK for the correct answer.

(10) birds **(2ND BOX)**
Award 1 MARK for the correct answer.

(11) he; it
Award 1 MARK for BOTH correctly identified PRONOUNS.

(12) conscientiously
Award 1 MARK for the correct ADVERB formed from CONSCIENCE.
DO NOT ACCEPT misspellings.

(13) who repaired my car **(2ND BOX)**
Award 1 MARK for the correct answer.

(14) as a noun phrase **(2ND BOX)**
Award 1 MARK for the correct answer.

(15) Maurice, my cousin, can speak... → certainty;
...that story could be... → possibility;
Jim might be asleep... → possibility;
I will apologise to Iris... → certainty
Award 1 MARK for ALL 4 correct answers.

(16) colon

Award 1 MARK for the correct answer.
ALSO ACCEPT plausible misspellings.

(17) <u>Even though Jennie was good at rounders</u> → subordinate clause;
<u>whenever it was possible</u> → subordinate clause;
<u>who coached her</u> → subordinate clause
Award 1 MARK for ALL 3 correct answers.

(18) **As** I had...;
When I checked...;
...my journey **until** the trains...
Award 1 MARK for ALL 3 correctly identified CONJUNCTIONS.

(19) bravery = courage
Award 1 MARK for BOTH correctly identified SYNONYMS.

(20) We've been waiting since six o'clock. **(2ND BOX)**
Award 1 MARK for THE ONE correctly identified sentence.

(21) *Answers will differ for each part of this question.*
Award 1 MARK for a GRAMMATICALLY CORRECT and CORRECTLY PUNCTUATED sentence that uses 'PROMISE' as a NOUN.
Example:
- *I made her a solemn <u>promise</u>.*
DO NOT ACCEPT answers that change the given form of the noun. Example: Alex always keeps his <u>promises</u>.

Award 1 MARK for a GRAMMATICALLY CORRECT and CORRECTLY PUNCTUATED sentence that uses 'PROMISE' as a VERB.
Example:
- *I <u>promise</u> to be good.*
DO NOT ACCEPT answers that change the given form of the verb. Example: I <u>have promised</u> to be good.

(22) look **(1ST BOX)**
Award 1 MARK for the correct answer.

(23) liberate ≠ confine; responsible ≠ undependable; insincere ≠ genuine; assist ≠ hinder
Award 1 MARK for ALL 4 correct answers.

(24) *Answers will differ, but MUST all be GRAMMATICALLY CORRECT, CONTAIN A SUBORDINATE CLAUSE and be CORRECTLY PUNCTUATED. Example:*
- *Louise and Jo<u>, who are best friends,</u> swam in the sea.*
Award 1 MARK for a correct answer.
DO NOT ACCEPT punctuation mistakes; the use of a phrase instead of a subordinate clause; or the addition of another main clause.

(25) <u>Sandra</u> → S (subject); <u>gave</u> → V (verb); <u>it</u> → O (object)
Award 1 MARK for ALL 3 correct answers.

(26) marie is **french**, but she also speaks **german. she** has

lived in **berlin** since **april**, 2012.
Award 1 MARK for ALL 6 correct answers.

(27) The slippery road caused an accident. **(2ND BOX)**
Award 1 MARK for the correct answer.

(28) The play was very good — brilliant, in fact — so it was no surprise that the audience applauded loudly. **(3RD BOX)**
Award 1 MARK for the correct answer.

(29) 3RD BOX
The correct place for the dash is as follows: The team knew exactly what would happen — their striker would be sent off.
Award 1 MARK for the correct answer.

(30) Claire has visited Greece several times. **(1ST BOX)**
Award 1 MARK for the correct answer.

(31) When you see Jake, tell him about the party. **(4TH BOX)**
Award 1 MARK for the correct answer.

(32) Mike informed Janet, "I know where your book has been left."
Award 1 MARK for the correct answer.

(33) One of the five retired **racehorses,** which were being auctioned last **weekend,** won the Grand National ten years ago.
Award 1 MARK for BOTH correctly placed COMMAS.

(34) ...see you <u>later</u> → adverb;
...my <u>best</u> jacket → adjective;
...bird sang <u>sweetly</u> → adverb;
...girl was <u>lonely</u> → adjective
Award 1 MARK for ALL 4 correct answers.

(35) *Answers will differ, but MUST all FULLY EXPLAIN BOTH SENTENCES. Example:*
- *The first sentence means that the children who received prizes happened to be in Year 6. The second sentence means that ALL the children who were in Year 6 received prizes.*

Award 1 MARK for A FULL EXPLANATION OF BOTH SENTENCES.
ALSO ACCEPT answers that are not written in full sentences.
DO NOT ACCEPT answers that explain only one sentence or which explain the use of the comma in general.

(36) I have an up-to-date version of that software. **(3RD BOX)**
Award 1 MARK for the correct answer.

(37) *Answers will differ, but MUST all be CORRECTLY PUNCTUATED SENTENCES that CORRECTLY USE THE PASSIVE VOICE. Examples:*
- *They were chased.*
- *They were chased across the field by the angry bull.*

Award 1 MARK for a correct answer.
DO NOT ACCEPT answers which change the verb or the tense.

(38) ...school <u>until</u> she has... → subordinating conjunction;

...here <u>until</u> the doctor... → subordinating conjunction;
...busy <u>until</u> the end... → preposition
Award 1 MARK for ALL 3 correct answers.

(39) *Answers will differ for some nouns, but they MUST all be CORRECTLY SPELT. Examples:*
- *truth → truthful OR truthless*
- *coward → cowardly*
- *debate → debated OR debatable*
- *feather → feathery OR featherless OR feather-like*
- *man → manly OR manlike OR mannish.*

Award 1 MARK for 5 correct answers.
ALSO ACCEPT answers using capital letters.

(40) <u>although</u> → subordinating conjunction;
<u>When</u> → subordinating conjunction;
<u>so</u> → co-ordinating conjunction
Award 1 MARK for ALL 3 correct answers.

(41) *Answers will differ. Example:*
- *Is it necessary that she <u>go</u> there?*

Award 1 MARK for a correct answer.
DO NOT ACCEPT answers using capital letters.

(42) Ten; their; this
Award 1 MARK for ALL 3 correct answers.

(43) all of Lady Herbert's valuable paintings and jewels
Award 1 MARK for the correct FULL NOUN PHRASE.

(44) has become
Award 1 MARK for the correct answer.

(45) *Answers will differ, but MUST all be CORRECTLY PUNCTUATED. Example:*
- *You need the following things to make a kite: a heavy-duty plastic bag, electrical tape, a line, a plastic winder and 2 rods.*

Award 1 MARK for a correctly punctuated LIST.
ALSO ACCEPT answers which correctly separate the items using semi-colons; contain misspellings; and that change the order of the items in the list.
DO NOT ACCEPT answers omitting any item or listing the items using bullet points.

(46) *Answers will differ. Example:*
- *Sally is a friend of <u>mine</u>.*

Award 1 MARK for a correct answer.
DO NOT ACCEPT answers that use a possessive determiner and a noun, e.g. my sister's.

(47) often
Award 1 MARK for the correct answer.

(48) That author's books are always **exciting:** each one she has written is full of thrilling adventures.
Award 1 MARK for the correctly placed COLON.

(49) full stop **(4TH BOX)**
Award 1 MARK for the correct answer.

(1) Where did she go Tuesday before last **(2ND BOX)**
Award 1 MARK for the correct answer.

(2) I must admit that I find geography rather **boring;** history is far more interesting.
Award 1 MARK for the correctly inserted SEMI-COLON.

(3) When Ali came to London, he visited Hampton Court. **(4TH BOX)**
Award 1 MARK for the correct answer.

(4) to work together **(3RD BOX)**
Award 1 MARK for the correct answer.

(5) has finished **(3RD BOX)**
Award 1 MARK for the correct answer.

(6) ...we <u>are</u> putting...;
I <u>am</u> playing...;
friend, <u>are</u> in charge...
Award 1 MARK for ALL 3 correct answers.

(7) Last year, all of my classmates and I **(1ST BOX)**
Award 1 MARK for the correct answer.

(8) The rise of the robots — a dire consequence foreseen by the Professor — happened more swiftly than anticipated. **(2ND BOX)**
Award 1 MARK for the correct answer.

(9) determiner **(4TH BOX)**
Award 1 MARK for the correct answer.

(10) 3RD BOX
The correct place for the dash is as follows: We finally learned the secret that the old beggar had kept hidden so well — he was a very rich man.
Award 1 MARK for the correct answer.

(11) adjectives **(4TH BOX)**
Award 1 MARK for the correct answer.

(12) Polly sneezed as she pulled down the box: it was covered with dust and cobwebs. **(4TH BOX)**
Award 1 MARK for the correct answer.

(13) That is a particularly <u>fast</u> sports car. **(2ND BOX)**
Award 1 MARK for the correct answer.

(14) The nearest city (San Paolo) is two hours away. **(3RD BOX)**
Award 1 MARK for the correct answer.

(15) Helen's great-grandfather fought in World War II. **(1ST BOX)**

Award 1 MARK for the correct answer.

(16) *Answers will differ, but MUST all be a GRAMMATICALLY CORRECT and CORRECTLY SPELT SUBORDINATING CONJUNCTION. Example:*
* *I never go swimming <u>after</u> I've had a heavy meal.*
Award 1 MARK for a correct answer.

(17) What a ridiculous idea to have **(4TH BOX)**
Award 1 MARK for the correct answer.

(18) "You have no <u>right</u> to say that!" exclaimed Cyril. **(2ND BOX)**
Award 1 MARK for the correct answer.

(19) **Selma (whose** two brothers joined our **school) has** just started training to become a dental surgeon.
Award 1 MARK for the correctly inserted PAIR OF BRACKETS.

(20) <u>Bill and Ben</u> had to... → They;
...to find <u>Ralph</u> → him
Award 1 MARK for BOTH correct answers.
DO NOT ACCEPT 'They' without a capital letter in this instance (i.e. 'they').

(21) Sheila asked Hassan, "Do you like that Renaissance painting?" **(3RD BOX)**
Award 1 MARK for the correct answer.

(22) If only Juan were here, he would know what to do. **(1ST BOX)**
Award 1 MARK for the correct answer.

(23) Phoebe <u>who sings in the choir</u> lives on my road. **(4TH BOX)**
Award 1 MARK for the correct answer.

(24) lazy = idle
Award 1 MARK for BOTH correctly identified SYNONYMS.

(25) It's really cold... → apostrophe used for a contracted form;
...the book's cover → apostrophe used for possession;
...seen Noel's bag → apostrophe used for possession;
...that's the correct... → apostrophe used for a contracted form
Award 1 MARK for ALL 4 correct answers.

(26) You're not leaving the table until you've finished your food! **(3RD BOX)**
Award 1 MARK for the correct answer.

(27) Read all of this book by the beginning of next term **(4TH BOX)**
Award 1 MARK for the correct answer.

(28) Dervla **Murphy** is an **Irish** travel writer who has always been fascinated by distant **lands. She** cycled around the **Irish** countryside when she was **young. She** has now visited places much farther away, including **Ethiopia** and **Peru.**
Award 1 MARK for the correct insertion of ALL the CAPITAL LETTERS and FULL STOPS.

(29) Firemen, who rescue people trapped in **buildings, are** extremely brave and deserve all our gratitude.
Award 1 MARK for the correctly inserted PAIR OF COMMAS.

(30) to decide → decides OR has decided;
to open → opened
Award 1 MARK for 2 correct answers.

(31) *Answers will differ, but MUST all be a GRAMMATICALLY CORRECT and CORRECTLY PUNCTUATED COMMAND that uses the IMPERATIVE. Example:*
• *To begin with, work out how much spaghetti you need.*
Award 1 MARK for a correct answer.

(32) After they came top of their year → S (subordinate);
Layla started studying at university → M (main);
Paulina got a job working for a famous tech company → M (main)
Award 1 MARK for ALL 3 correct answers.

(33) or; Although; If
Award 1 MARK for ALL 3 correct answers.

(34) Kenneth raced down the stairs. **(1ST BOX)**;
Yesterday, we went to our favourite cinema. **(2ND BOX)**
Award 1 MARK for BOTH correct answers.

(35) ducks **(3RD BOX)**
Award 1 MARK for the correct answer.

(36) Two Saturdays **ago,** we watched an extremely exciting match between Everton and **Liverpool — the** last of the season.
Award 1 MARK for the correctly placed COMMA and correctly placed DASH.

(37) who
Award 1 MARK for the correct answer.

(38) to be → is;
to do → does;
to tell → tell
Award 1 MARK for ALL 3 correct answers.
DO NOT ACCEPT any misspellings of the verb forms.

(39) Most of the books on this **bookshelf — all** the ones about ancient **Greece — belong** to my sister Celia.
Award 1 MARK for the correctly placed PAIR OF DASHES.

(40) dis- OR dis
Award 1 MARK for the correct PREFIX.

(41) willing ≠ reluctant

Award 1 MARK for BOTH correctly identified ANTONYMS.

(42) mine
Award 1 MARK for the correct answer.

(43) full stop **(4TH BOX)**
Award 1 MARK for the correct answer.

(44) The large <u>friendly</u> dog wagged its tail when it saw me. The fairy was delighted by her new <u>friendship</u> with the elf.
Award 1 MARK for BOTH correct answers derived from the word FRIEND.
DO NOT ACCEPT misspellings.

(45) I don't believe Sonia's story as she tends to <u>exaggerate</u> everything.
Award 1 MARK for the correct VERB.
DO NOT ACCEPT misspellings.

(46) The brilliant concert pianist Anita Jacobs who is famous all over the world also happens to be my aunt's **sister-in-law.**
Award 1 MARK for the TWO correctly inserted HYPHENS.

(47) *Answers will differ, but MUST all be a CORRECTLY PUNCTUATED SENTENCE written in the PASSIVE VOICE. Example:*
• *The exotic flowers were being watered.*
Award 1 MARK for a correct answer.
ALSO ACCEPT the following:
• *The exotic flowers were being watered by the gardener.*

(48) had enjoyed → have enjoyed;
had been → has been
Award 1 MARK for BOTH correct answers.
DO NOT ACCEPT misspellings.

(49) *Answers will differ, but MUST all be an appropriate NOUN PHRASE that is made up of AT LEAST THREE WORDS. Example:*
• <u>*The waiting fans*</u> *cheered wildly when they saw the famous film star.*
Award 1 MARK for a correct answer.

(50) quite
Award 1 MARK for the correct answer.

(1) civil → ized; energy → etic; wonder → ous
Award 1 MARK for ALL 3 correct answers.

(2) Now the exam is over, you may leave **whenever** you are ready, **though** you must hand in your answers first.
Award 1 MARK for ALL 3 correctly inserted CONJUNCTIONS.

(3) football *OR* our favourite football
Award 1 MARK for a correct answer.

(4) The restaurant had ____ kinds of drinks. → all;
Eve said she didn't want ____ fruit juice. → any;
She had ____ iced tea instead. → some
Award 1 MARK for ALL 3 correct answers.

(5) Mary begged to go swimming **(2ND BOX)**
Award 1 MARK for the correct answer.

(6) Some people wear uniforms to work, such as doctors and nurses; other people, such as teachers and journalists, do not. **(4TH BOX)**
Award 1 MARK for the correct answer.

(7) *Answers will differ, but MUST all be CORRECTLY SPELT. Example:*
- *The new exhibition is meant to be* stunning.
Award 1 MARK for the correct insertion of an appropriate ADJECTIVE.

(8) 2ND BOX & **4TH BOX**
The correct places for the missing apostrophes are as follows: The train to Leeds is late: its driver's been delayed by problems with his car's engine.
Award 1 MARK for BOTH correct answers.

(9) Just after the heavy thunderstorm **ended,** a rainbow appeared.
Award 1 MARK for the correctly inserted COMMA.

(10) ...Sue is really enjoying... → present progressive;
She was not looking... → past progressive;
...she is finding... → present progressive
Award 1 MARK for ALL 3 correct answers.

(11) ...friend of Jason's and Tilly's → theirs;
...helped Jason and Tilly build... → them
Award 1 MARK for BOTH correct PRONOUNS.

(12) She's a well-meaning but accident-prone girl. **(1ST BOX)**
Award 1 MARK for the correct answer.

(13) Omar said he would help me. **(3RD BOX)**
Award 1 MARK for the correct answer.

(14) All the guests should... → question;
All the guests are expected... → statement;
What amazing presents... → exclamation;
If you are a guest... → command
Award 1 MARK for ALL 4 correct answers.

(15) Neither of those dresses fits me anymore. **(4TH BOX)**
Award 1 MARK for the correct answer.

(16a) dashes *OR* a pair of dashes
Award 1 MARK for a correct answer.

(16b) commas *OR* a pair of commas *OR* brackets *OR* a pair of brackets
Award 1 MARK for a correct answer.

(17) ...said she's been... → she has;
...thinks they'll do... → they will *OR* they shall;
...Rana should've arrived... → should have
Award 1 MARK for ALL 3 correct answers.

(18) There should be inverted commas before the word 'said'. **(2ND BOX)**
There should be a comma after the word 'Hercules'. **(4TH BOX)**
Award 1 MARK for BOTH correct answers.

(19) The Great Fire of London started in Pudding Lane. **(1ST BOX)**
Award 1 MARK for the correct answer.

(20) Crosswords are great **fun:** they are a source of entertainment and relaxation at the same time.
Award 1 MARK for the correctly placed COLON.

(21) body **(4TH BOX)**
Award 1 MARK for the correct answer.

(22) shoes'
Award 1 MARK for the correct answer.

(23) Many people's devices... → commas used correctly;
Oscar likes having... → commas used incorrectly;
Before you leave... → commas used incorrectly;
You can have... → commas used correctly
Award 1 MARK for ALL 4 correct answers.

(24) beside; on
Award 1 MARK for BOTH correct answers.

(25) Were Mira and Jessie frightened by the noise?
Award 1 MARK for the correct answer.

(26) have; used
Award 1 MARK for BOTH correct answers.

(27) who's visiting us at the moment;
which is not far from here;
that I go to the most
Award 1 MARK for ALL 3 correct answers.

(28) whilst; so
Award 1 MARK for BOTH correct answers.

(29) <u>You should visit the Tower of London</u>... → main clause;
...<u>as we may be back late tonight</u> → subordinate clause;
...<u>that was being broadcast that evening</u>... → subordinate clause
Award 1 MARK for ALL 3 correct answers.

(30a) After they'd eaten the **fish,** the sharks and the dolphins swam off.
Award 1 MARK for the correctly placed COMMA.

(30b) After they'd **eaten,** the **fish,** the sharks and the dolphins swam off.
Award 1 MARK for BOTH correctly placed COMMAS.
DO NOT ACCEPT the use of a serial comma: After they'd eaten, the fish, the <u>sharks,</u> and the dolphins swam off.

(31) *Answers will differ, but must CORRECTLY explain the MEANINGS of the verbs 'IMPROVED' and 'DISPROVED'. Examples:*
• *This argument must be <u>improved</u>. → This means that the argument must be <u>made better</u>.*
• *This argument must be <u>disproved</u>. → This means that the argument must be <u>shown to be false</u>.*
Award 1 MARK for BOTH correct EXPLANATIONS.

(32) when; that
Award 1 MARK for BOTH correct answers.

(33) ...to <u>you</u> → yours;
...to <u>Mr and Mrs Mason</u> → theirs;
...to <u>my brother and me</u> → ours
Award 1 MARK for ALL 3 correct answers.

(34a) *Answers will differ. Example:*
• *Antonyms are words that have opposite meanings.*
Award 1 MARK for a correct DEFINITION.

(34b) *Answers will differ. Example:*
• *agitated.*
Award 1 MARK for a correct ANTONYM.

(35) whip → is whipping; grease → are greasing; reassess → is reassessing
Award 1 MARK for ALL 3 correct answers.
DO NOT ACCEPT misspellings of any of the verb forms.

(36) justice → just; law → lawful
Award 1 MARK for BOTH correct ADJECTIVES.
DO NOT ACCEPT misspellings of the adjectives.

(37) whom **(1ST BOX)**
Award 1 MARK for the correct answer.

(38) *Answers will differ for each part of this question. Award 1 MARK for a GRAMMATICALLY CORRECT and CORRECTLY PUNCTUATED sentence that uses 'AIM' as a VERB. Example:*
• *I <u>aim</u> to be there by 6 o'clock.*
DO NOT ACCEPT answers that change the given form of the verb. Example: We <u>are aiming</u> to be on time.

Award 1 MARK for a GRAMMATICALLY CORRECT and CORRECTLY PUNCTUATED sentence that uses 'AIM' as a NOUN. Example:
• *The <u>aim</u> of the exercise is to learn something.*
DO NOT ACCEPT answers that change the given form of the noun. Example: I have two <u>aims</u> in life.

(39) Rob ... is my neighbour.
Award 1 MARK for the FULL correct answer.

(40) Last week, our electricity supply was... → passive voice;
This was caused by... → passive voice;
The power was restored... → passive voice
Award 1 MARK for ALL 3 correct answers.

(41) *Answers will differ, but MUST all be a CORRECTLY PUNCTUATED sentence in the PASSIVE VOICE. Examples:*
• *We were beaten.*
• *We were beaten in the final.*
• *We were beaten in the final by last year's champions.*
Award 1 MARK for a CORRECTLY PUNCTUATED sentence in the PASSIVE VOICE.

(42) friendless; lonely
Award 1 MARK for BOTH correct answers.

(43) a preposition phrase **(2ND BOX)**
Award 1 MARK for the correct answer.

(44) were **(4TH BOX)**
Award 1 MARK for the correct answer.

(45) an exclamation **(3RD BOX)**
Award 1 MARK for the correct answer.

(46) I have warned you of the consequences. **(4TH BOX)**
Award 1 MARK for the correct answer.

(1) How wonderful that we've won the cup **(3RD BOX)**
Award 1 MARK for the correct answer.

(2) You will need several things for the school camping trip next **week:** sleeping bags, a few cooking utensils, waterproof jackets, Wellington boots and several warm sweaters.
Award 1 MARK for the correctly inserted COLON.

(3) As he loves English history, Ed's bought a book about the Stuarts. **(4TH BOX)**
Award 1 MARK for the correct answer.

(4) between stars **(1ST BOX)**
Award 1 MARK for the correct answer.

(5) isn't running **(2ND BOX)**
Award 1 MARK for the correct answer.

(6) Sandy **doesn't** know...;
...Bob **doesn't** really...;
If Eric **doesn't** apologise...
Award 1 MARK for ALL 3 correct answers.

(7) Hearing a loud yell, Rupert stopped **(1ST BOX)**
Award 1 MARK for the correct answer.

(8) I feel really awful about the misunderstanding; however, I have no idea how it happened — honestly, I don't. **(3RD BOX)**
Award 1 MARK for the correct answer.

(9) adjective **(4TH BOX)**
Award 1 MARK for the correct answer.

(10) 4TH BOX
The correct place for the dash is as follows: Ella heaved a huge sigh of relief as she finally wrapped the last of her daughter's birthday presents — she'd finished!
Award 1 MARK for the correct answer.

(11) adverbs **(3RD BOX)**
Award 1 MARK for the correct answer.

(12) The knight refused all help; he was determined to travel alone. **(2ND BOX)**
Award 1 MARK for the correct answer.

(13) These boxes fold <u>flat</u> for storage. **(2ND BOX)**
Award 1 MARK for the correct answer.

(14) Our trip — and a very long trip it was, too — took over 12 hours. **(3RD BOX)**
Award 1 MARK for the correct answer.

(15) Kobo the Magician will not be performing this coming Friday. **(4TH BOX)**
Award 1 MARK for the correct answer.

(16) *Answers may differ, but MUST all contain an appropriate SUBORDINATING CONJUNCTION. Example:*
- *Vijay will be punished if his bad behaviour continues.*
Award 1 MARK for a correct answer.

(17) If you go swimming, remember to take your goggles **(1ST BOX)**
Award 1 MARK for the correct answer.

(18) Tears were streaming <u>down</u> the princess's face. **(4TH BOX)**
Award 1 MARK for the correct answer.

(19) My older **cousin, Stefan,** who lived in Glasgow before he moved to Durham with his parents when he was **ten,** is a brilliant guitarist and an accomplished saxophonist.
Award 1 MARK for ALL 3 correctly inserted COMMAS.

(20) the instructions... → them;
the box... → it
Award 1 MARK for BOTH correct answers.

(21) The teacher asked, "Do any of you know who discovered gravity?" **(2ND BOX)**
Award 1 MARK for the correct answer.

(22) It is essential that the work be done by tomorrow. **(3RD BOX)**
Award 1 MARK for the correct answer.

(23) I think I would be very tired <u>if I were the headmaster</u>. **(4TH BOX)**
Award 1 MARK for the correct answer.

(24) stubborn ≠ flexible
Award 1 MARK for BOTH correctly identified ANTONYMS.

(25) Tomorrow, we're having... → apostrophe used for a contracted form;
Liam's coughing... → apostrophe used for possession;
The knight's armour... → apostrophe used for possession;
Paula's been to... → apostrophe used for a contracted form
Award 1 MARK for ALL 4 correct answers.

(26) The Cornish cave which was used by smugglers has been flooded. **(2ND BOX)**
Award 1 MARK for the correct answer.

(27) She can't help us, can she **(3RD BOX)**
Award 1 MARK for the correct answer.

(28) My brother speaks fluent **French** although he's never had **lessons. I** have been studying it for five years and still find it difficult to speak the **language. My German,** however, is much better than **his.**
Award 1 MARK for the correct insertion of ALL the CAPITAL LETTERS and FULL STOPS.

(29) The tour guide told us that ancient Roman **frescoes (especially** those which are to be found in the famous city of **Pompeii) are** notable sources of information about ancient Roman painting.
Award 1 MARK for the correctly inserted PAIR OF BRACKETS.

(30) to kidnap → had kidnapped *OR* kidnapped;
to interfere → interfere *OR* are interfering
Award 1 MARK for 2 correct answers.

(31) *Answers will differ, but MUST all be a GRAMMATICALLY CORRECT and CORRECTLY PUNCTUATED COMMAND that uses the IMPERATIVE. Example:*
• *First, go to your nearest tube station.*
Award 1 MARK for a correct answer.

(32) A priceless, medieval manuscript was found → M (main);
while the local library was being refurbished → S (subordinate);
it is now on display in the Town Hall → M (main)
Award 1 MARK for ALL 3 correct answers.

(33) if; yet; whenever
Award 1 MARK for ALL 3 correct answers.

(34) *A Passage to India* is a famous English novel. **(2ND BOX)**;
My brothers and I travelled together during the summer. **(4TH BOX)**
Award 1 MARK for BOTH correct answers.

(35) herd of cows **(3RD BOX)**
Award 1 MARK for the correct answer.

(36) I watched a programme about a young maths **genius:** a teenager from a small Greek island I'd never heard of **before — it** was remarkable!
Award 1 MARK for the correctly placed COLON and correctly placed DASH.

(37) whose
Award 1 MARK for the correct answer.

(38) to offer → has offered;
to find → has found;
to have → has had
Award 1 MARK for ALL 3 correct answers.
DO NOT ACCEPT any misspellings of the verb forms.

(39) Mr Robert Davenport is a keen **sailor, as** well as a bit of an amateur **comedian, who** rows across the English Channel twice each year.

Award 1 MARK for the correctly placed PAIR OF COMMAS.

(40) de- *OR* de
Award 1 MARK for the correct PREFIX.

(41) contaminated = polluted
Award 1 MARK for BOTH correctly identified SYNONYMS.

(42) yours
Award 1 MARK for the correct answer.

(43) semi-colon **(4TH BOX)**
Award 1 MARK for the correct answer.

(44) Beth always behaves <u>calmly</u> during a crisis.
The giant <u>calmed</u> down once the mouse disappeared.
Award 1 MARK for BOTH correct answers derived from the word CALM.
DO NOT ACCEPT misspellings.

(45) "Stop that right now! You <u>are embarrassing</u> me!" hissed Juliana.
Award 1 MARK for the correct VERB.
ALSO ACCEPT have embarrassed OR will embarrass OR are going to embarrass.
DO NOT ACCEPT misspellings.

(46) Ali's history teacher told that him he'd written a **well-thought-out** essay which was full of interesting information and persuasive arguments about the English Civil War.
Award 1 MARK for BOTH correctly inserted HYPHENS.

(47) *Answers will differ, but MUST all be a CORRECTLY PUNCTUATED SENTENCE written in the PASSIVE VOICE. Example:*
• *The wrong bus has been caught.*
Award 1 MARK for a correct answer.
ALSO ACCEPT any of the following:
• *The wrong bus has been caught by mistake.*
• *The wrong bus has been caught by Phil and Gina by mistake.*
• *The wrong bus has been caught by mistake by Phil and Gina.*

(48) irons → has been ironing;
whistles → has been whistling
Award 1 MARK for BOTH correct answers.
DO NOT ACCEPT misspellings.

(49) *Answers will differ, but MUST all be an appropriate NOUN PHRASE that is made up of AT LEAST THREE WORDS. Example:*
• *In honour of his bravery, the fireman was given a medal by <u>the grateful mayor</u>.*
Award 1 MARK for a correct answer.

(50) wide
Award 1 MARK for the correct answer.

(1) picture → esque; astronomy → ical; decision → ive
Award 1 MARK for ALL 3 correct answers.

(2) Though the performance had been short, yet the audience applauded loudly as it had been brilliant.
Award 1 MARK for ALL 3 correctly inserted CONJUNCTIONS.

(3) match OR the match
Award 1 MARK for a correct answer.

(4) _____ books look interesting. → these;
I think I'll buy _____ one about snakes. → the;
They don't have _____ copies left. → many
Award 1 MARK for ALL 3 correct answers.

(5) What a thing to ask of me **(3RD BOX)**
Award 1 MARK for the correct answer.

(6) Later, he realised the truth: right from the start, he had never wanted to study engineering. **(1ST BOX)**
Award 1 MARK for the correct answer.

(7) *Answers will differ, but MUST all be CORRECTLY SPELT.*
Example:
• *They arrived late for their appointment.*
Award 1 MARK for the correct insertion of an appropriate ADVERB.

(8) 3RD BOX & 4TH BOX
The correct places for the missing inverted commas are as follows: Charles sheepishly admitted to his wife, "I can't remember where I've parked the car!"
Award 1 MARK for BOTH correct answers.

(9) Near the hermit's hut was a river that eventually flowed into a **lake:** the Waters of Forgetfulness and Peace.
Award 1 MARK for the correctly inserted COLON.

(10) The orchestra has been rehearsing... → present perfect progressive;
...members had been worrying... → past perfect progressive;
...they have been spending... → present perfect progressive
Award 1 MARK for ALL 3 correct answers.

(11) ...my cousin and me... → us;
Aunt Paige, my cousin and I... → we
Award 1 MARK for BOTH correct PRONOUNS.

(12) He was proud of his family's three-hundred-year-old name. **(4TH BOX)**
Award 1 MARK for the correct answer.

(13) As I'm highly qualified, I may get the job. **(2ND BOX)**
Award 1 MARK for the correct answer.

(14) Once you've bought the tickets... → command;
How excited Jane will be... → exclamation;
When the tickets have been bought... → statement;
After you've bought the tickets... → question
Award 1 MARK for ALL 4 correct answers.

(15) I realised I'd forgotten my phone charger at home. **(3RD BOX)**
Award 1 MARK for the correct answer.

(16a) brackets OR a pair of brackets
Award 1 MARK for a correct answer.

(16b) dashes OR a pair of dashes OR commas OR a pair of commas
Award 1 MARK for a correct answer.

(17) That does not look... → doesn't;
...you had better... → you'd;
...we will not be able... → won't
Award 1 MARK for ALL 3 correct answers.

(18) There should be an exclamation mark after the word 'thief'. **(1ST BOX)**;
There should be inverted commas before the word 'Stop', not 'thief'. **(5TH BOX)**
Award 1 MARK for BOTH correct answers.

(19) Queen Elizabeth I succeeded her sister, Queen Mary I, in 1558. **(4TH BOX)**
Award 1 MARK for the correct answer.

(20) My grandmother's favourite saying was 'Never a lender nor a borrower **be'**; her least favourite saying of all was 'Every cloud has a silver lining'.
Award 1 MARK for the correctly placed SEMI-COLON.

(21) boundary **(2ND BOX)**
Award 1 MARK for the correct answer.

(22) we're
Award 1 MARK for the correct answer.

(23) The Italian dish... → semi-colon used incorrectly;
Surprised to see me... → semi-colon used incorrectly;
The name of the band... → semi-colon used incorrectly;
There was only one word... → semi-colon used incorrectly
Award 1 MARK for ALL 4 correct answers.

(24) During; on; beneath
Award 1 MARK for ALL 3 correct answers.

(25) Has Otto been studying for three hours?
Award 1 MARK for the correct answer.

(26) were; perform
Award 1 MARK for BOTH correct answers.

(27) Unless someone comes to my rescue;
if you wake up early enough;
even though it is very difficult
Award 1 MARK for ALL 3 correct answers.

(28) so; before
Award 1 MARK for BOTH correct answers.

(29) After he had decided to grow vegetables in his garden,... → subordinate clause;
...which caused an immense amount of damage → subordinate clause;
...I'm right → main clause
Award 1 MARK for ALL 3 correct answers.

(30a) As they'd promised **Alex,** Betty and Shelly came to the party.
Award 1 MARK for the correctly placed COMMA.

(30b) As they'd **promised, Alex,** Betty and Shelly came to the party.
Award 1 MARK for BOTH correctly placed COMMAS.
DO NOT ACCEPT the use of a serial comma: As they'd promised, Alex, Betty, and Shelly came to the party.

(31) *Answers will differ, but must CORRECTLY explain the MEANINGS of the verbs 'ANTEDATES' and 'POSTDATES'. Examples:*
- *This civilization antedates the ancient Greeks. → This means that this civilization came into existence before the ancient Greeks.*
- *This civilization postdates the ancient Greeks. → This means that this civilization came into existence after the ancient Greeks.*
Award 1 MARK for BOTH correct EXPLANATIONS.

(32) neither; nor
Award 1 MARK for BOTH correct answers.

(33) ...to Stuart and Bart → theirs;
...to me → mine;
...to Khaled → his
Award 1 MARK for ALL 3 correct answers.

(34a) *Answers will differ. Example:*
- *Synonyms are words that mean the same thing.*
Award 1 MARK for a correct DEFINITION.

(34b) *Answers will differ. Example:*
- *exaggeration.*
Award 1 MARK for a correct SYNONYM.

(35) cough → has been coughing; suffer → has been suffering; plan → have been planning
Award 1 MARK for ALL 3 correct answers.
DO NOT ACCEPT misspellings of any of the verb forms.

(36) indignation → indignantly; fury → furiously
Award 1 MARK for BOTH correct ADVERBS.
DO NOT ACCEPT misspellings of the adverbs.

(37) whose **(4TH BOX)**
Award 1 MARK for the correct answer.

(38) *Answers will differ for each part of this question.*
Award 1 MARK for a GRAMMATICALLY CORRECT and CORRECTLY PUNCTUATED sentence that uses 'CONTRACT' as a VERB. Example:
- *I don't want to contract a cold this winter.*
DO NOT ACCEPT answers that change the given form of the verb. Example: I contracted a nasty cold last winter.

Award 1 MARK for a GRAMMATICALLY CORRECT and CORRECTLY PUNCTUATED sentence that uses 'CONTRACT' as a NOUN. Example:
- *The lawyer gave her a contract to sign.*
DO NOT ACCEPT answers that change the given form of the noun. Example: Some contracts have been stolen from the office.

(39) that was designed by Joseph Paxton and Owen Jones in the nineteenth century
Award 1 MARK for the FULL correct answer.

(40) Annoyingly, the concert... → passive voice;
Everyone who had bought... → active voice;
None of us know... → active voice
Award 1 MARK for ALL 3 correct answers.

(41) A large bumblebee stung Elias.
Award 1 MARK for a CORRECTLY PUNCTUATED sentence in the ACTIVE VOICE.
ALSO ACCEPT A large bumblebee stung Elias while he was sunbathing.

(42) again; tiresomely
Award 1 MARK for BOTH correct answers.

(43) as a fronted adverbial **(2ND BOX)**
Award 1 MARK for the correct answer.

(44) be **(1ST BOX)**
Award 1 MARK for the correct answer.

(45) a question **(3RD BOX)**
Award 1 MARK for the correct answer.

(46) According to her teachers at school, Ola is doing extremely well. **(2ND BOX)**
Award 1 MARK for the correct answer.

Printed in Great Britain
by Amazon